RECIPES AND STORIES FROM THE
SLAP YA MAMA FAMILY

EXPANDED EDITION

THE WALKER FAMILY

83 press

Copyright ©2025 by 83 Press

All rights reserved. No part of this book may be reproduced or transmitted in any form or by any means, electronic or mechanical, including photocopying, or by any information storage and retrieval system, without permission in writing from 83 Press. Reviewers may quote brief passages for specific inclusion in a magazine or newspaper.

83 Press
2323 2nd Ave North
Birmingham, AL 35203

ISBN: 979-8-9923852-0-5
Printed in China

GROWING UP CAJUN

RECIPES AND STORIES FROM THE
SLAP YA MAMA FAMILY
EXPANDED EDITION

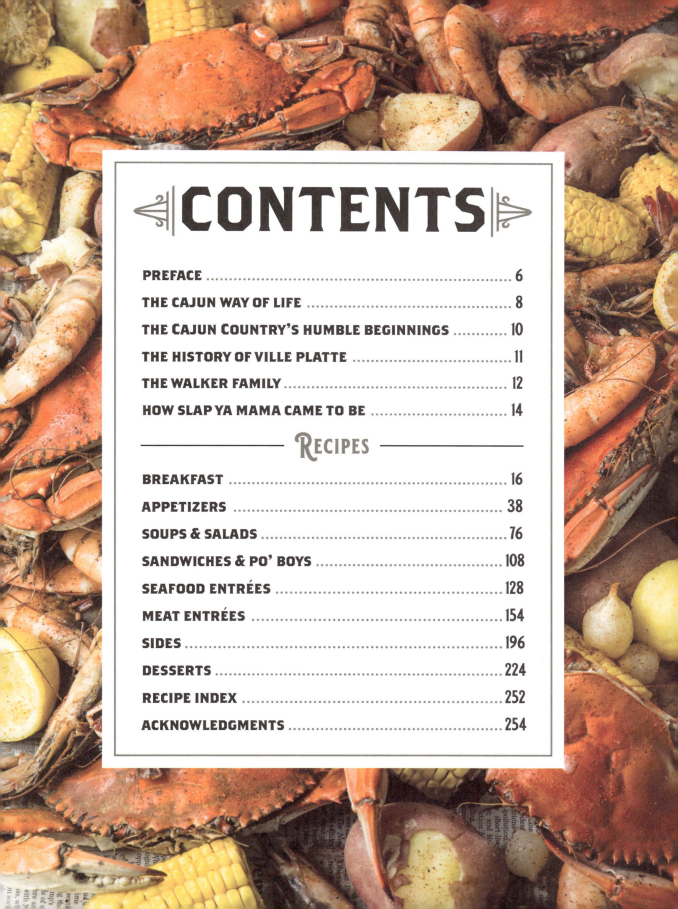

CONTENTS

PREFACE 6
THE CAJUN WAY OF LIFE 8
THE CAJUN COUNTRY'S HUMBLE BEGINNINGS 10
THE HISTORY OF VILLE PLATTE 11
THE WALKER FAMILY 12
HOW SLAP YA MAMA CAME TO BE 14

RECIPES

BREAKFAST 16
APPETIZERS 38
SOUPS & SALADS 76
SANDWICHES & PO' BOYS 108
SEAFOOD ENTRÉES 128
MEAT ENTRÉES 154
SIDES 196
DESSERTS 224
RECIPE INDEX 252
ACKNOWLEDGMENTS 254

PREFACE

While being raised in a Cajun household is a unique experience all on its own, the one constant that never fails to appear in all our favorite stories is the food. Just the smell of our Maw Maw's pecan pie is powerful enough to instantly bring us back to everything the dessert represents. Whether it was a holiday, a family gathering, or just a Saturday spent with friends eating crawfish, we knew when that pie made its appearance on the kitchen table, that day would be a special one.

From the time we were born, all our experiences were set against the backdrop of a rich culture that was all we knew. Our family gatherings were joyful occasions spent with music, laughter, and everyone pitching in to create a delicious meal. For us, happiness and food went hand in hand, and we knew no separation between the two. It wasn't until we left Ville Platte for college that we realized not everyone lived in a world quite like ours. Many of our new friends found it intriguing and were instantly drawn to it. Through the Slap Ya Mama company, we've had the opportunity to share what we know with the rest of the world: Food is love, and Cajun food is pure joy.

Growing up in Cajun Country gave us the treasured foundation upon which we built our adult lives. We shared some of that culture in our cookbook, *Growing Up Cajun*. After the overwhelming support for our first cookbook, we're excited to share this expanded collection of recipes and family stories with you. Inside, you'll find the dishes you've grown to love along with a new chapter dedicated to our favorite breakfast options and more than 30 never-before-seen family recipes. We hope this edition will make you feel like part of our family and inspire you to make new memories—and meals—with your own loved ones.

-Jack and Joe Walker

THE CAJUN WAY OF LIFE

On a breezy Sunday afternoon in March, TW and Jennifer (Mama Jen) gather their family and friends for a backyard crawfish boil in their small town of Ville Platte, Louisiana. Their 2-year-old granddaughter, Andi, leaps out of the car and runs into their arms. She takes a curious look inside the crawfish pot and then darts away from the wiggling mudbugs. Upbeat and down-home zydeco and swamp pop tunes play from a speaker perched on a bright red convertible, and Jennifer stomps her cowboy boots in rhythm to the music. TW and Jennifer's sons, Jack and Joe, catch up with old friends over bottles of beer as they wait for the water to boil. Joe's wife, Tana, keeps an eye on Andi while tending to their baby, Ruby Grace, who attracts a crowd of doting ladies.

With a big smile on his face, TW takes in the scene around him, sharing a moment from his childhood in his warm Cajun accent. "We were sitting around like this when I was a kid, and my daddy said, 'I wonder what the poor people are doing.' I said, 'Dad, I thought we were poor.' And he said, 'If you can do this with family and friends, all these different generations, you're not poor.'"

Louisiana's Cajun Country is home to one of the richest cultures in the United States. In the middle of the state—cradled between the mighty Mississippi River and the Texas border and lying some 150 miles northwest of New Orleans—Ville Platte's rural landscape ranges from low-lying crawfish ponds and mossy cypress bayous to grassy hills where horses graze.

Many of Ville Platte's residents are descendants of French-Canadian immigrants, exiled from Acadia by the British Crown in 1755. In search of a new home, the Acadians started a new life along Louisiana's bayous. Little did they know they were also starting one of the most distinctive and authentic cultures in the US—the Cajun culture, which remains strong more than 250 years later.

Small-town country life meant Cajun families had to create their own entertainment. They worked hard during the day and then gathered around food and music at night with relatives, neighbors, and travelers. They lived off the land, using what was available to them. Some combination of crawfish, shrimp, pork, chicken, rice, and the "holy trinity" of green bell pepper, onion, and celery comprised most every dish. They cooked big pots of gumbo and étouffée, and played the accordion, violin, and guitar. But while Cajuns are known for their joie de vivre culture of loving life and having a good time, above all else, they value God and family.

For the Love of Cooking

The Walkers are a close-knit family, bound by their love of Cajun food and culture. Married for more than 40 years, TW and Jennifer each grew up with parents who were great cooks, and they have passed their love of Cajun cuisine onto their own sons.

"Everything revolved around the kitchen in the evening," recalls TW. "The kids would come in and do their school work, and we always had a family meal together. That's where the boys learned to cook. They would stir the pot because we were stirring the pot."

The Walkers didn't just have your typical kitchen set up—they had multiple kitchens. Jack and Joe's childhood home near Bayou Chicot featured a traditional indoor kitchen as well as an outdoor kitchen and a barbecue shed. Later, when the Walkers moved into town, TW relocated and renovated a decrepit home on the property to serve as the family's outdoor kitchen and party house. There sits the Walker's year-round Christmas tree right next to their jukebox, which plays their favorite oldies, like "La Porte d'en Arrière," the traditional Cajun Mardi Gras song—and the only song TW will get up and dance to.

"The kitchen brings all the family together," says Jennifer. "We are all cooking. We drink and party and listen to music. We're always having a good time."

From the time Jack and Joe were just 3 years old, they remember cooking with their mom and dad, surrounded by friends and family, and ready to share a fresh pot of whatever was on the stove. They tagged along with TW on hunting trips and learned how to make Squirrel Sauce Piquante. After a long day of Mardi Gras revelry, they brought their friends back to the house for a generous pot of Chicken and Sausage Gumbo. Every Easter, they went crawfishing with their cousins in local ponds and, at night, ate pound after pound of mudbugs while standing elbow to elbow. Each Christmas, they served heaping pans of Jambalaya along with their World-Famous Atomic Potatoes, Mama Jen's Cajun Cornbread, and a variety of tasty dips (since every family member had a favorite).

This special family, who has always loved to cook and entertain, was destined to make the Cajun culture known. Through their strong bond with one another in the kitchen and at the dinner table, they have helped put their small town of Ville Platte on the map.

> "EVERYTHING REVOLVED AROUND THE KITCHEN IN THE EVENING."
> —TW

A Taste of Cajun Culture

Through their Slap Ya Mama Cajun products, the Walker family has seasoned the world with their zesty culture. What started as a homemade Cajun seasoning created in their kitchen became a world-renowned household brand. From seasoning and hot sauce to fish fry and étouffée, "Slap Ya Mama" is now stamped proudly on more than a dozen products offered at gas stations, grocery stores, and restaurants on three continents.

While the bright red, yellow, and green packaging and its bold name are no doubt eye-catching, rest assured that no one has ever slapped their mama in Ville Platte, except for a loving slap on the back. Jennifer, who came up with the name, was inspired by one of the dishes TW is most known for, his World Famous Slap Ya Mama Atomic Potatoes.

In the pages that follow, you'll learn more about how Slap Ya Mama came to be. You'll get to know all about the Walker family and their Cajun way of life through stories and recipes that span generations. The Walkers will take you through making family favorites and Cajun specialties, like Fried Boudin Balls, Turtle Soup, Debris Po' Boys, Blackened Red Fish, and Boiled Crawfish with all the sides and sauces. Remember to save room for dessert, because you won't want to miss Maw Maw's Pecan Pie, Bananas Foster, Bread Pudding, and the Best Chocolate Chip Cookies.

"We just want to share our culture, our heritage, and the fun we have in the kitchen," says Jack. "More than anything, food has had the biggest impact on our lives—it always brings our friends and family together."

So, no matter where you are in the country or the world, gather your friends and family, crank up the swamp pop, and bring a little taste of Cajun Country to your table.

The Cajun Country's Humble Beginnings

From the 1500s to the 1700s, European countries played a game of hot potato in the New World. Territory changed hands quickly, but for a time, France occupied much of what is now Canada and the middle of North America, England ruled much of the East Coast, and Spain claimed Florida and much of the Southwest, from Louisiana to California and Mexico.

In the early 1600s, country folk from western France began making a life for themselves in Acadia—which is in today's Nova Scotia, Canada. As the French settlers adapted to the New World, they became known as Acadians. In 1713, the area swapped from French to British hands when the Treaty of Utrecht was signed. The treaty meant the Acadians were now subjects of the British monarchy and were expected to worship at the Church of England. The faithful Acadians refused to pledge fealty to either the British crown or Anglican religion, and rebelled. In 1755, the British governor decided to solve the problem of unruly Acadians by forcibly dispersing them in Le Grand Dérangement. The Acadian refugees were scattered across the British territories and colonies, and many lost their lives.

Exiled Acadians wandered the New World looking for a home. Preferring to follow a Catholic king, many traveled to the Spanish territory of Louisiana, just west of French New Orleans and 2,000 miles from their Canadian home. Spain allowed the refugees to settle in their territory, so more Acadians flocked there in hopes of reuniting with their families and communities in the Louisiana countryside. These Acadians adapted to their new home and became known as Cajuns.

The most famous Acadian refugee is the fictious character Evangeline, the heroine of Henry Wadsworth Longfellow's poem of the same name. Evangeline was separated from her love, Gabriel, in the expulsion and searched her entire life for him across the New World until they finally reunited as he died in her arms. Of the 22 parishes in Louisiana's Cajun Country, one is named Evangeline, and Ville Platte is the parish seat.

In the 1700s, Spain's El Camino Real de los Tejas linked the territory with Texas and Mexico City. Because the Acadians were unwanted exiles themselves, they met strangers with open arms and warm hospitality. The frequently traveled trail fostered relationships among Native Americans and Irish, Spanish, and French immigrants, creating a rich gumbo of cultures and a distinctive dialect.

In this part of the country, English names are far less common than names like LeBlanc, Landry, Hebert (pronounced A-bair), Boudreaux, and Fontenot. Locals mix French right in with their English, and in many schools, French language immersion begins in kindergarten.

Cajuns are known for zydeco music, played with an accordion, washboard, guitar, and violin, and swamp pop, which combines R&B, country/Western, and traditional French Louisiana music. In the 1950s and 1960s, legendary producer Floyd Soileau recorded several swamp pop hits at his Ville Platte studio, which the state later proclaimed the Swamp Pop Capital of the World.

But Cajuns are most famous for their food, which should not be confused with Creole cuisine. While the two have similarities, they possess defining differences. Cajuns hail from the French territory of Acadia and live in Louisiana's rural areas, while Creoles live in New Orleans and are a mix of Spanish, French, Caribbean, and African American ancestry. Thus, Creole food is considered city food, while Cajun food is more simple, country-style food.

Typical Cajun food includes chicken and sausage gumbo, deep-fried pork cracklin's, crawfish étouffée, jambalaya, and boudin (sausage stuffed with rice, green onions, and seasonings). With every bite, this delectable culture is relished and preserved.

THE HISTORY OF VILLE PLATTE
EST. 1824

PHOTO COURTESY OF BOBBY DARDEAU OF *BONNES NOUVELLES*

The area around Ville Platte was first settled in the 1780s, and it joined the United States in the famous Louisiana Purchase of 1803. Louisiana became a state in 1812 but continued operating under the Napoleonic code, a civil and legal system created by the French. It's still the only state in the country with parishes instead of counties.

Ville Platte's unique name likely came from a mistake that just stuck. Surveyors on the low-lying land had to use pirogues (narrow canoes) and flat boats to do their work properly, so they referred to the area as "Flat Ville," or "Flat Town." When translated to French, both should be Ville Plat, but wound up Ville Platte.

In 1824, Major Marcellin Garand, a local celebrity who fought in Napoleon's Grande Armée, bought one of the first plots of land in the area and consequentially became the founder of Ville Platte. He built a shop and tavern on the land, which attracted travelers on their way to El Camino Real de los Tejas, and in 1842, he became Ville Platte's first postmaster. Major Garand also introduced the European sport of jousting that remains a fixture today.

Ville Platte was incorporated on March 16, 1858, by an act of the Louisiana legislature that was written in both French and English. Residents of Ville Platte and the surrounding area were—and are today—predominantly Catholic. The first Catholic church in Ville Platte was established in 1854, along with a Catholic school. In 1900, the town's population was just over 160. In 1907, the railroad came through town, boosting the population. In 1911, Ville Platte became the parish seat of Evangeline Parish, and in 1930, Main Street was paved. In 1939, Chicot State Park—Louisiana's largest—was founded, and in the 1940s, oil was discovered there, bringing some buzz to the small town.

Ville Platte is now home to more than 6,000 residents and remains entrenched in colorful Cajun culture. The people there are proud of who they are and where they came from. The community's yearly festivals include Mardi Gras in nearby Mamou, the Louisiana Cotton Festival, Squirrel Day, the Smoked Meat Festival, and the Le Louisiana Tournoi de Ville Platte jousting tournament.

Driving into town from Highway 167, two claims to fame are stamped onto the welcome sign: "Swamp Pop Music Capital of the World" and "Smoked Meat Capital of the World." Today, Ville Platte could add a third: "Home to Slap Ya Mama Cajun Products."

THE WALKER FAMILY

In 1956, Anthony Walker (or TW, as he's best known to his friends) was born the youngest of three boys in Ville Platte. "My dad was born and raised in St. Landry—he was an Americ*an*," TW says, with an emphasis on the last syllable. "That's why I have the Walker name. It's a little outside of the Cajun Country, but he married a Cajun girl, who was a Fontenot."

His mother, Wilda, was known as one of the best cooks in the family, and his father, W.R., often boiled crawfish and barbecued, so TW and his brothers learned the ins and outs of cooking.

TW met his wife-to-be, Jennifer Fontenot, when she was 13. He crashed her eighth-grade party, and Jennifer, who was raised Catholic, interviewed him for a school project about what it was like to be Baptist. TW must have had some good answers because they started going steady after that and eventually got married.

The couple was—and remains—popular in their hometown of Ville Platte. TW became an attorney, and Jennifer worked as a hair stylist before she took over at the family store. Their oldest son, Jack, was named after his great-great-grandfather, Andrew Jackson Walker. Born just a few years later, their second son, Joseph William Walker (Joe Willy), was named after TW's favorite quarterback, Joseph William Namath.

Now grandparents, TW's parents became Maw Maw and Paw Paw Dub. His good buddies Big Wade and Little Gary became Mr. Big Wade and Mr. Little Gary to the boys. TW hosted his own Wednesday supper clubs just for the guys, where all the men helped out in the kitchen.

TW and Jennifer also hosted many gatherings together and spent leisurely weekend afternoons around food. The Ville Platte way is to extend an open invitation to friends, a casual "let's get together Friday night and cook something." On these occasions, the guests are just as involved in the kitchen as their hosts—everyone stirring the pot and contributing to the meal. It was in this communal environment that one of the world's most famous Cajun products was born.

HOW SLAP YA MAMA CAME TO BE

Serving customers in the family store's deli, Jennifer was disappointed in their store-bought seasoning. She went home and complained to TW, and they went to work making their own.

"We went to the store and got all kinds of different seasonings, and we started mixing it at home until it was something we wanted," says Jennifer. "Really all we put in it was salt, black pepper, red pepper, and garlic. We got the proportions like we wanted—not too salty—and put it in an old pickle jar." Then she enlisted her sons for help. Jack and Joe, who were 15 and 13, respectively, at the time, rolled the jar back and forth in the house's only carpeted room until the mixture was perfectly combined.

The Walkers started using the seasoning in the deli, and soon, customers wanted to buy it. "So, we got jars from the dollar store," says Jennifer. "They had little handles and shakers. The boys made labels off the computer that said 'Slap Your Mama, Bayou Chicot, Louisiana,' since that's where we lived at the time. We put them on the counter and sold them for a dollar, and people kept buying them."

Soon, the Walkers had to buy in bulk. They went to Targil Seasoning & Butcher Supplies in the nearby town of Opelousas and made 25 pounds of their seasoning. They sold out of that, too. Their customers and friends were using it like salt and pepper on everything from popcorn, French fries, and scrambled eggs to their favorite Cajun foods. They encouraged the Walkers to sell to a larger audience, but in order to do so, they'd need to create a barcode and get the product approved. "We got to the point where we asked each other, 'Are we gonna do this for real?'" Jennifer says.

Their product had been perfected, but they first had to settle on the name. TW, an attorney and Southern gentleman, said they couldn't name it Slap Your Mama, "because the little old ladies are gonna get mad." Jennifer insisted it was the name that would sell their product, but she wanted to make one change first.

"We're going to change it to Slap Ya Mama because it's much more inviting and fun to say," says Jennifer. TW compromised, and certainly not wanting to offend his own mother, he included the following story on every product: "In 1956, Wilda Marie Fontenot Walker gave birth to the creator of this award-winning seasoning blend. Every time she uses it, she receives a loving slap on the back and a kiss on the cheek, thanking her for another great-tasting Cajun dish."

With that, the Walkers were ready for business. They ordered 200 cases with the revised Slap Ya Mama name, and they debuted their new product at Ville Platte's Smoked Meat Festival. They sold 18 cases that weekend, and the following Monday, Jennifer loaded the rest into her little Nissan 280 ZX sports car and went door-to-door from grocery stores to convenient stores. Her area soon expanded to Lafayette and Alexandria, and TW bought her a minivan to fit more product. If a store manager said no, Jennifer gave them a case for free and insisted, in her sweet Cajun accent, that they just see what their customers thought. Sure enough, the stores sold out and were calling her to order 10 cases at a time.

"A lot of people buy it because of the name, but they buy that second can because of the flavor," says TW's brother Bob. At the time, Bob was selling Slap Ya Mama products at East Mississippi Community College where he worked—the only place east of the Mississippi you could find it at the time.

Meanwhile, Jack and Joe had finished high school and were packing their bags for LSU, 90 minutes away in Baton Rouge. "When we took off to go to college, Slap Ya Mama was in its premature stages," says Joe. "We had no idea what the potential would be, where it was going to go, and if we could see our future in it."

A few years after the dot-com boom, Jack and Joe created a website for the company and started taking online orders. Between classes, their studies, college parties, and their part-time jobs at a local restaurant, they packaged and shipped Slap Ya Mama seasoning. "We drove to Ville Platte once a week during college to pick up product and bring it back," recalls Jack. "We had two closets in our downstairs living room stocked full with Slap Ya Mama. You'd walk in the door and would smell the spices. We hired our roommate to work for us, and our friends walked around campus and wore Slap Ya Mama T-shirts." Unaware of the exceptional entrepreneurs in her midst, a neighbor thought they were selling some sort of illegal substance through UPS. "Just a whole bunch of seasoning," they assured her.

"Once we got to where we were going to graduate, more and more packages were going out the door," says Joe. "We saw the potential in it and thought, 'Wow, we really started something, and it's growing.'"

In 2007, the boys moved back home to Ville Platte to run the family business. Jennifer had connected with a distributor who had gotten their product into Texas, Arkansas, and all over Louisiana, and their footprint was rapidly expanding. Jack and Joe loaded their suitcases and attended international food shows, sharing their homegrown brand with the world.

Today, Slap Ya Mama is sold in the United States and exported to more than 20 plus countries. The Walkers are running their impressive global business with just 12 employees, and the family remains heavily involved. Joe and his wife, Tana, take care of distribution and bookkeeping from Ville Platte, while Jack manages the sales and marketing from his office in New Orleans. Although TW is officially retired from the practice of law and the family business, he continues to help with the legal matters, real estate deals, and contracts. Targil, just up the highway, still makes many of the Slap Ya Mama seasoning products.

Jennifer and TW get their family together often to cook and test new products in their outdoor kitchen in Ville Platte, relying on the advice of their most loyal and enthusiastic customers—their close friends and family, including their own mamas.

CHAPTER ONE
BREAKFAST

Start each day with a Cajun kick

CRAWFISH-POTATO OMELET

MAKES 3

Pillowy, soft eggs are filled with hash browns, crawfish tails, tasso, cheese, and just the right amount of Cajun heat.

- 1½ tablespoons vegetable oil
- 2¼ cups frozen diced hash browns with peppers and onion
- 2 tablespoons chopped celery
- ¼ cup chopped tasso ham
- 1 cup crawfish tails, drained
- 2 tablespoons chopped green onion
- 2 teaspoons Slap Ya Mama Cajun Pepper Sauce
- 9 large eggs, divided
- ¾ teaspoon kosher salt, divided
- 3 tablespoons unsalted butter, divided
- ⅔ cup shredded sharp white Cheddar cheese
- Garnish: sliced green onion
- Slap Ya Mama Original Blend Cajun Seasoning and Slap Ya Mama Cajun Pepper Sauce, to serve

1. In a 9-inch nonstick skillet with sloped sides, heat oil over medium-high heat. Carefully add hash browns and celery. Cover and cook, stirring occasionally, until golden brown, about 6 to 8 minutes. (Reduce heat to medium if potatoes are becoming too brown.) Stir in tasso; cook for 1 minute. Stir in crawfish, green onion, and Slap Ya Mama Cajun Pepper Sauce. Reduce heat to medium. Cook, stirring occasionally, for 2 minutes. Spoon into a bowl. Wipe skillet, and let cool, about 5 minutes.

2. For each omelet: In a medium bowl, whisk together 3 eggs and ¼ teaspoon salt. Melt 1 tablespoon butter in same skillet over medium-low heat. Add whisked egg mixture, and cook, without stirring, until edges are set. Using a spatula, gently lift up cooked edges so that uncooked portion flows underneath; cook until center is just set. Spoon one-third of crawfish mixture onto one side of omelet. Sprinkle with about 3 tablespoons cheese. Using a spatula, fold other side of omelet over crawfish filling. Gently slide omelet onto a plate. Repeat two more times with remaining eggs, salt, butter, crawfish mixture, and cheese. Garnish with green onion, if desired. Serve with Slap Ya Mama Original Blend Cajun Seasoning and Slap Ya Mama Cajun Pepper Sauce.

Saturday Cartoons AND PAIN PERDU

Born in 1956, TW grew up as a big fan of Saturday morning cartoons. To him, there was nothing more exciting than waking up early, and rushing to the living room to turn on the black-and-white TV. Bugs Bunny, Rocky and Bullwinkle, and Mighty Mouse filled the screen, but his absolute favorite show was *Jonny Quest*.

As much as Tony loved those cartoons, there was something he loved even more—something that made those Saturday mornings truly special. It was the sweet aroma drifting through the house, signaling that his mother, Wilda Marie, was in the kitchen making "lost bread." The Cajuns called the dish *pain perdu*, but to Tony, the name didn't matter. It was pure magic.

Wilda Marie would take stale bread—bread that might have otherwise been thrown away—and transform it into the most delicious breakfast treat. Fresh eggs, sugar, vanilla, cinnamon, and milk were blended together, creating a rich, velvety mixture that soaked deep into the bread before sizzling in a hot pan. The scent of caramelized sugar and warm spices wrapped around Tony like a comforting hug.

Tony, however, wasn't the only one drawn to the kitchen by the irresistible smell. His two older brothers, Bobby and Ken, were just as eager for a plate of their mother's pain perdu. More often than not, Tony had to fight to make sure he got his fair share before his bigger, faster brothers devoured it all. It was a friendly but fierce competition, with each of them trying to grab the crispiest, most golden pieces before they disappeared.

Sitting cross-legged on the floor, plate in hand, Tony savored every bite while watching his favorite cartoons. The crispy edges, the soft, custard-like center, and the dusting of sugar made each mouthful unforgettable.

Those Saturday mornings, with cartoons on the screen, his brothers at his side, and Wilda Marie's pain perdu on his plate, remained some of his fondest childhood memories—simple, warm, and filled with love.

It was those cherished memories that later inspired the creation of Kiss Ya Mama Cinnamon Sugar. The Walkers wanted to capture that same comforting sweetness—the perfect blend of cinnamon and sugar that turned a simple breakfast into something magical. Every sprinkle of Kiss Ya Mama Cinnamon Sugar brings back those Saturday mornings, sitting in front of the TV, enjoying his mother's homemade pain perdu. Now, families everywhere can create their own special moments, just like Tony did all those years ago.

CINNAMON SUGAR DOUGHNUTS

MAKES ABOUT 10

There's nothing like a fresh, warm doughnut to start the day. For an easier morning, make the dough the night before and let it rise overnight in the refrigerator.

½	cup warm water (105° to 110°)	½	cup unsalted butter, melted and cooled slightly
4	tablespoons granulated sugar, divided	2	large eggs, room temperature
1	(0.25-ounce) package active dry yeast	¼	cup bread flour
4 to 4¼	cups all-purpose flour, divided	1½	teaspoons kosher salt
¾	cup whole milk, room temperature	1	teaspoon vanilla extract
		1	container Kiss Ya Mama Cinnamon Sugar

1. In the bowl of a stand mixer, stir together ½ cup warm water, 1 tablespoon sugar, and yeast by hand. Let stand until foamy, about 10 minutes.

2. Add 2 cups all-purpose flour, milk, melted butter, eggs, bread flour, salt, vanilla, and remaining 3 tablespoons sugar to yeast mixture; beat at low speed with paddle attachment just until combined. Add 2 cups all-purpose flour; beat at low speed until well combined, about 1 minute.

3. Switch to the dough hook attachment; beat at medium-low speed until dough starts to pull away from sides of bowl, 4 to 6 minutes, adding up to remaining ¼ cup all-purpose flour, 1 tablespoon at a time, if needed. (Dough will still be quite soft and slightly sticky but should not seem excessively wet.)

4. Spray a large bowl with cooking spray. Place dough in bowl, turning to grease top. Cover and let rise in a warm, draft-free place until doubled in size, 40 minutes to 1 hour. (Alternatively, cover and let rise in refrigerator overnight. When ready to use, proceed as directed.)

5. Spray 3 large baking sheets with cooking spray. Cut out 10 (6-inch) squares of parchment paper, and place on prepared pans. Spray parchment with cooking spray. Spray 3 large sheets of plastic wrap with cooking spray.

6. Punch down dough; turn out onto a heavily floured surface, and roll or pat to ½-inch thickness. Using a 3½-inch doughnut cutter dipped in flour, cut dough. Gently transfer doughnuts to prepared parchment squares, spacing at least 2 to 2½ inches apart. Reroll scraps once, and let stand for 5 to 10 minutes; cut scraps. Cover doughnuts with prepared plastic wrap, spray side down, and let rise in a warm, draft-free place until puffed, 40 minutes to 1 hour.

7. In a large heavy-bottomed pot, pour oil to a depth of 2 inches, and heat over medium heat until a deep-fry thermometer registers 365°. Line 2 large rimmed baking sheets with paper towels. Place cinnamon sugar blend in a medium shallow bowl.

8. Working in batches, use parchment paper to gently pick up doughnuts and add to oil (it is OK if parchment goes into oil; just remove quickly). Fry until golden brown, about 1 minute per side. Using a spider strainer, transfer doughnuts to prepared pans. Let drain slightly. Immediately toss in Kiss Ya Mama Cinnamon Sugar. Place on a wire rack.

PAW PAW BEV'S BISCUITS

MAKES ABOUT 10

A family favorite, these biscuits are the perfect start to every morning.

- 2 cups all-purpose flour
- 2 teaspoons baking powder
- 1 teaspoon sugar
- ½ teaspoon kosher salt
- ½ cup vegetable oil spread, softened
- ½ cup whole milk

1. Preheat oven to 400°.
2. In a large bowl, whisk together flour, baking powder, sugar, and salt. Using fingertips, work vegetable oil spread into flour. Pour in milk and stir until just combined. Turn out on a floured surface and knead together until well combined. Using a rolling pin, roll out dough to ¾-inch thickness. Cut with a 3-inch biscuit cutter dipped in flour. Place on a greased baking sheet.
3. Bake until lightly golden brown, 18 to 20 minutes.

BLOODY MARY BOARD

MAKES 8

Here's the best way to wake up after a night out on the town in New Orleans. Instead of serving individual cocktails, make a large pitcher and have everyone garnish their own glass.

1   (32-ounce) bottle Slap Ya Mama Bloody Mary Mix
12   ounces vodka
Lemon wedges
Slap Ya Mama Chili Lime Signature Seasoning
Ice
Garnish: Cane Syrup-Candied Bacon (see page 30), lemon wedges, lime slices, celery stalks, pickled okra, olives

1. In a large pitcher, stir together Slap Ya Mama Bloody Mary Mix and vodka. Place the pitcher on a tray with 8 (16-ounce) glasses, lemon wedges, Slap Ya Mama Chili Lime Signature Seasoning, ice, and garnishes.
2. When ready to serve, pour Slap Ya Mama Chili Lime Signature Seasoning in shallow dish. Wet the rim of each glass with a lemon wedge and dip into seasoning. Fill each glass halfway with ice. Pour Slap Ya Mama Bloody Mary Mix mixture over ice. Garnish with Cane Syrup-Candied Bacon, lemon wedges, lime slices, celery stalks, pickled okra, and olives, if desired.

BEIGNETS

MAKES ABOUT 20

No trip to New Orleans is complete without this famous treat. Fluffy and coated in powdered sugar, you'll be transported to Louisiana with each bite.

½ cup warm water (105° to 110°)
3 tablespoons plus 1 teaspoon granulated sugar, divided
1 teaspoon active dry yeast
2 tablespoons all-vegetable shortening
½ teaspoon kosher salt
½ cup boiling water
½ cup evaporated milk
1 large egg
4 to 5 cups all-purpose flour
Peanut oil, for frying
Garnish: confectioners' sugar

1. In a small bowl, stir together ½ cup warm water, 1 teaspoon granulated sugar, and yeast. Let stand until mixture is foamy, about 5 minutes.
2. In the bowl of a stand mixer fitted with the paddle attachment, beat shortening, salt, and remaining 3 tablespoons granulated sugar at medium speed until smooth. Add ½ cup boiling water and evaporated milk, beating until combined. Add egg, beating until combined. Stir in yeast mixture. Gradually add 4 cups flour, beating until a dough forms.
3. Switch to the dough hook attachment. Beat at medium speed until dough pulls away from sides of bowl, about 6 minutes, adding remaining 1 cup flour as needed. (Dough should be smooth, elastic, and slightly sticky.)
4. Spray a large bowl with cooking spray. Place dough in bowl, turning to grease top. Cover and refrigerate for at least 30 minutes or up to 2 hours.
5. On a lightly floured surface, roll dough into a 14x12-inch rectangle, about ¼ inch thick. Using a sharp knife, cut dough into 2½-inch squares. (Do not reroll dough.)
6. In a 7-quart enameled-coated cast-iron Dutch oven, pour oil to a depth of 3 inches, and heat over medium-high heat until a deep-fry thermometer registers 370°. Working in batches, fry dough, turning frequently, until golden brown, 2 to 3 minutes. Carefully remove from hot oil, and let drain on paper towels. Sprinkle with confectioners' sugar, if desired. Serve warm.

CREOLE TOMATO BREAKFAST SANDWICHES

MAKES 3

Cane Syrup-Candied Bacon is the star of this sandwich. The spicy, sweet flavor is the perfect companion to the classic flavors of a rich fried egg and fresh ripe tomato.

- ½ cup mayonnaise
- 2 tablespoons Creole mustard
- 2 teaspoons Slap Ya Mama Hot Blend Cajun Seasoning
- 2 teaspoons grated garlic
- 2 teaspoons fresh lemon juice
- 2 tablespoons unsalted butter
- 3 large eggs
- Kosher salt, to taste
- Ground black pepper, to taste
- 3 Paw Paw Bev's Biscuits (see page 24)
- 3 thick slices Creole tomato
- 6 slices Cane Syrup-Candied Bacon (recipe follows)

1. In a medium bowl, whisk together mayonnaise, mustard, Slap Ya Mama Hot Blend Cajun Seasoning, garlic, and lemon juice until well combined.
2. In a medium skillet, melt butter over medium heat. Gently crack eggs into skillet. Season to taste with salt and pepper. Cover and fry until whites are set and yolks are desired degree of doneness, 3 to 4 minutes. Transfer to a plate.
3. Cut biscuits in half, and spread about 1 tablespoon mayonnaise mixture on each half. Divide tomato, bacon, and eggs over bottom halves of biscuits. Cover with tops of biscuits. Serve immediately.

CANE SYRUP–CANDIED BACON
MAKES 12 SLICES

- 12 slices thick-cut center-cut bacon
- ½ cup firmly packed dark brown sugar
- ¼ cup cane syrup
- 2 tablespoons apple cider vinegar
- 2 teaspoons Slap Ya Mama Original Blend Cajun Seasoning
- 1 teaspoon Kiss Ya Mama Cinnamon Sugar

1. Preheat oven to 350°. Line 2 rimmed baking sheets with foil. Top with a wire rack; spray with cooking spray.
2. Place bacon on prepared wire racks.
3. Bake for 12 to 14 minutes. (Bacon will not be crisp.) Leave oven on.
4. Meanwhile, in a small saucepan, bring brown sugar, cane syrup, vinegar, Slap Ya Mama Original Blend Cajun Seasoning, and Kiss Ya Mama Cinnamon Sugar to a boil over medium heat, stirring frequently; cook for 1 minute. Lightly brush half of syrup mixture onto bacon.
5. Bake until just beginning to caramelize, about 10 minutes. Turn bacon, rearranging slices to ensure even baking. Lightly brush with remaining syrup mixture. Bake until caramelized, about 25 minutes more, turning, rearranging, and brushing with syrup mixture every 10 minutes. Transfer bacon to a piece of wax or parchment paper, and let cool slightly; serve warm.

CLASSIC CINNAMON ROLLS

MAKES 10

Nothing beats the sweet indulgence of a cinnamon roll. We took a classic recipe and made it even easier with our Kiss Ya Mama Cinnamon Sugar.

Dough:
- ¾ cup whole milk
- ½ cup water
- ⅓ cup unsalted butter, cubed
- 4 to 4¼ cups all-purpose flour, divided, plus more for dusting
- 2 tablespoons granulated sugar
- 1 tablespoon kosher salt
- 1 (0.25-ounce) package active dry yeast
- 1 large egg, room temperature

Filling:
- ½ cup unsalted butter, softened
- 1 container Kiss Ya Mama Cinnamon Sugar
- ½ teaspoon kosher salt

Glaze:
- ¼ cup whole buttermilk
- 2 ounces cream cheese, softened
- 2¼ cups confectioners' sugar
- ⅛ teaspoon vanilla extract

1. For dough: In a medium saucepan, heat milk and ½ cup water over medium heat to scalding. Remove from heat. Add butter; let stand, stirring occasionally, until butter is melted and an instant-read thermometer registers 120° to 130°.

2. In the bowl of a stand mixer, whisk together 2 cups flour, granulated sugar, salt, and yeast by hand. Add warm milk mixture; using the paddle attachment, beat at low speed until combined. Add egg, beating until combined. With mixer on low speed, gradually add 2 cups flour, beating just until a shaggy dough comes together and stopping to scrape sides of bowl.

3. Switch to the dough hook attachment. Beat at low speed until a soft, somewhat sticky dough forms, about 20 minutes, stopping to scrape sides of bowl and dough hook; add up to remaining ¼ cup flour, 1 tablespoon at a time, if dough is too sticky. Turn out dough onto a clean surface, and shape into a smooth round.

4. Lightly oil a large bowl. Place dough in bowl, turning to grease top. Cover and let rise in a warm, draft-free place until doubled in size, about 1 hour.

5. Lightly punch down dough. Cover and let stand for 10 minutes. Turn out dough onto a very lightly floured surface, and roll into an 18x12-inch rectangle.

6. For filling: Spread butter onto dough. Sprinkle with Kiss Ya Mama Cinnamon Sugar and salt, gently pressing into dough. Starting with one long side, roll dough into a log; pinch seam to seal. Place log seam side down, and cut into 10 rolls.

7. Spray a 10-inch cast-iron skillet with cooking spray. Place rolls in prepared skillet. Cover and let rise in a warm, draft-free place until doubled in size, 45 minutes to 1 hour.

8. Preheat oven to 350°.

9. Bake until golden brown and cooked through, 30 to 35 minutes. Let cool slightly in skillet.

10. For glaze: In a medium bowl, whisk together buttermilk and cream cheese until smooth. Add confectioners' sugar an d vanilla; beat until smooth. Spread glaze over warm rolls.

PAIN PERDU

MAKES ABOUT 6 SERVINGS

Whether covered in cane syrup or topped with fruit and whipped cream (or maybe all three), French toast is always a welcome sight.

- 5 large eggs, room temperature
- 1 cup whole milk
- 2 tablespoons Kiss Ya Mama Cinnamon Sugar, plus more to serve
- 1 teaspoon vanilla extract
- ½ teaspoon kosher salt
- 1 loaf brioche bread, cut into ¾-inch slices
- 6 tablespoons unsalted butter, divided

Sweetened whipped cream, cane syrup, and fresh fruit, to serve

1. In a medium shallow bowl, whisk together eggs, milk, Kiss Ya Mama Cinnamon Sugar, vanilla, and salt. Working in batches, dip bread slices into egg mixture, turning to coat each side. Remove immediately.
2. In a medium skillet, melt 2 tablespoons butter over medium-high heat. Add soaked bread to skillet, and cook until bread is golden brown, about 2 minutes per side. Repeat with remaining bread, using remaining egg mixture and butter.
3. To serve, top with whipped cream, Kiss Ya Mama Cinnamon Sugar, syrup, and fresh fruit. Best served warm.

KISS YA MAMA MUFFINS

MAKES 12

Filled with Kiss Ya Mama Cinnamon Sugar, each tender bite is loaded with tasty comfort.

- 2½ cups all-purpose flour
- 3½ teaspoons baking powder
- ¾ teaspoon kosher salt
- 1 cup granulated sugar
- ½ cup unsalted butter, melted and cooled slightly
- 2 large eggs, room temperature
- ¾ cup whole milk, room temperature
- ¼ cup sour cream, room temperature
- 1 teaspoon vanilla extract
- 18 teaspoons Kiss Ya Mama Cinnamon Sugar, divided

1. In a medium bowl, whisk together flour, baking powder, and salt.

2. In a large bowl, whisk together granulated sugar and melted butter. Whisk in eggs. Add milk, sour cream, and vanilla; whisk until smooth and combined. Gradually add flour mixture, whisking until almost combined. Using a small spatula, scrape sides of bowl; fold until no dry streaks remain. (There may be small lumps, but do not overmix the batter.) Cover and refrigerate for at least 1 hour, or up to overnight.

3. Preheat oven to 375°. Line cups of a 12-cup muffin pan with paper liners or spray with baking spray with flour.

4. Spoon 2 tablespoons batter into each cup. Top each with 1 teaspoon Kiss Ya Mama Cinnamon Sugar. Divide remaining batter among cups, about 3 tablespoons each; top each muffin with ½ teaspoon Kiss Ya Mama Cinnamon Sugar.

5. Bake for 10 minutes. Reduce oven temperature to 350°, and bake until golden and a wooden pick inserted in center comes out with a few moist crumbs, 10 to 12 minutes more. Let cool in pans for 10 minutes. Remove from pans, and let cool completely on a wire rack. Store in an airtight container for up to 3 days.

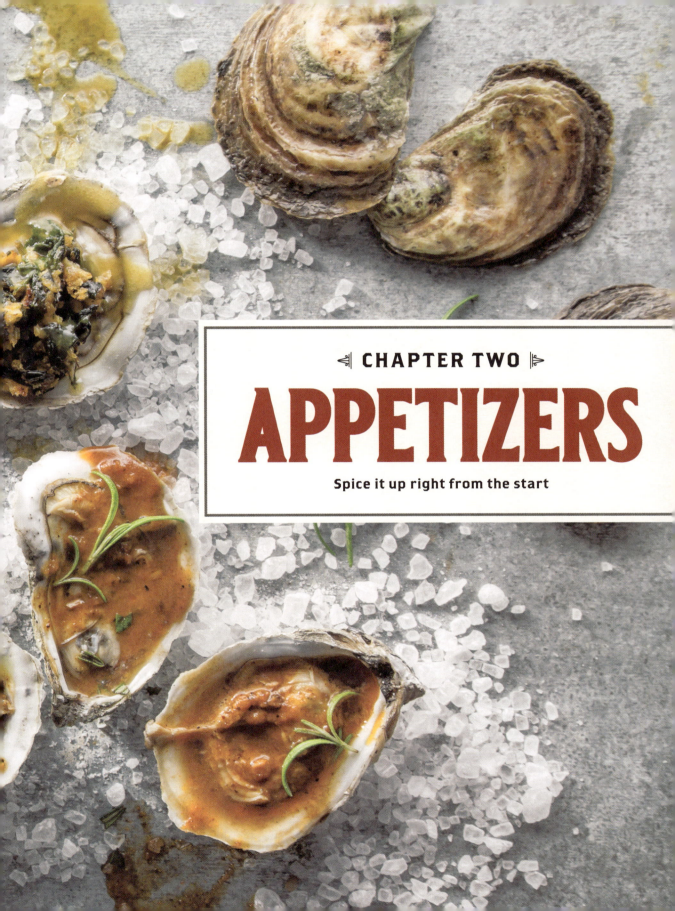

◀ CHAPTER TWO ▶

APPETIZERS

Spice it up right from the start

FRIED BOUDIN BALLS

MAKES 32

Perfect for passing around a family party or just frying up for fun, these bite-size boudin balls are deep-fried and seasoned with two famous Slap Ya Mama products.

1½   cups dry bread crumbs, plus more if needed
2   large eggs, lightly beaten
½   teaspoon kosher salt
¼   teaspoon Slap Ya Mama Hot Blend Cajun Seasoning
¼   teaspoon Slap Ya Mama Cajun Pepper Sauce, plus more to serve
1½   pounds pork boudin sausage, casings removed
Vegetable oil, for frying

1. In a shallow bowl, place bread crumbs. In another shallow bowl, whisk together eggs, salt, Slap Ya Mama Hot Blend Cajun Seasoning, and Slap Ya Mama Cajun Pepper Sauce.
2. Shape boudin sausage into 1¼-inch balls. Working in batches, dip balls in egg mixture, letting excess drip off. Roll in bread crumbs, coating evenly.
3. In a large Dutch oven, pour oil to a depth of 2 inches, and heat over medium-high heat until a deep-fry thermometer registers 360°. Fry balls, in batches, until light brown, 2 to 3 minutes. Let drain on paper towels. Serve warm with Slap Ya Mama Cajun Pepper Sauce.

COOKING TIP FROM MAMA JEN

Before starting to cook or bake, put on your favorite apron (mine is a Slap Ya Mama apron!) and your favorite music. Fix your favorite drink or glass of wine, and all of this will put you in the mood to cook.

STUFFED BELL PEPPERS

MAKES 6

You've never had bell peppers like these! Stuffed with fresh shrimp and lump crabmeat, these delicious starters are flavorful and baked to perfection.

- 6 medium green bell peppers
- ¼ cup unsalted butter
- ½ pound small fresh shrimp, peeled, deveined, and chopped
- ¼ cup diced onion
- ¼ cup diced green bell pepper
- 1 jalapeño, diced
- 2 cloves garlic, finely minced
- 2 tablespoons Slap Ya Mama White Pepper Blend Seasoning
- 8 to 10 dashes Slap Ya Mama Cajun Pepper Sauce
- ½ pound lump crabmeat
- 1½ cups shredded Cheddar cheese, divided
- ½ cup Italian bread crumbs
- 1 cup water

1. Preheat oven to 350°.
2. Cut tops off whole bell peppers, remove seeds, and rinse. In a large pot of water, boil bell peppers with a little salt for about 10 minutes. Drain, and set aside.
3. In a large skillet, combine butter, shrimp, onion, diced bell pepper, jalapeño, garlic, Slap Ya Mama White Pepper Blend Seasoning, and Slap Ya Mama Cajun Pepper Sauce. Cook over medium heat until shrimp are light pink in color, about 10 minutes. Add crabmeat, and sauté for 5 minutes. Remove from heat.
4. In a large bowl, stir together seafood mixture, 1 cup cheese, and bread crumbs until well combined and cheese is melted. Fill each bell pepper with mixture, and top with remaining ½ cup cheese.
5. Place bell peppers standing up in a shallow baking dish, making sure they don't fall over. Add 1 cup water to bottom of baking dish.
6. Bake, uncovered, for 30 to 35 minutes. Serve immediately.

MAMA JEN'S CAJUN CORNBREAD

MAKES 10 TO 12 SERVINGS

Of all her recipes, Mama Jen's Cajun Cornbread is probably her most recognized. Any time there is a family event, she makes her famous cornbread, and it isn't long before the whole tray is gone. You have to move quickly when she places her cornbread on the serving table, or you'll come up empty-handed.

- 1 tablespoon unsalted butter
- 1 cup diced smoked tasso or ham
- 1 cup diced smoked sausage
- 1 cup yellow cornmeal
- 1 tablespoon Slap Ya Mama Original Blend Cajun Seasoning
- 1 teaspoon baking soda
- 1 (14.75-ounce) can cream-style corn
- 1 cup whole milk
- ½ cup vegetable oil
- 2 large eggs, beaten
- 2½ cups shredded mild Cheddar cheese
- 1 small onion, finely chopped (about 1 cup)
- 1 medium green bell pepper, seeded and diced (about 1 cup)
- 3 medium jalapeños, seeded and minced (about ½ cup)

1. Preheat oven to 350°. Grease a 13x9-inch baking pan with butter.

2. In a medium skillet, cook tasso and sausage over medium-high heat, stirring frequently, until browned, 5 to 7 minutes. Set aside.

3. In a large bowl, stir together cornmeal, Slap Ya Mama Original Blend Cajun Seasoning, and baking soda using a fork. Add corn, milk, oil, and eggs, stirring until well combined. Add tasso, sausage, cheese, onion, bell pepper, and jalapeño, stirring until well combined. Spoon mixture into prepared pan.

4. Bake until a wooden pick inserted in center comes out clean and top is golden brown, about 55 minutes. Let cool for 30 minutes before serving.

DEVILED EGGS

MAKES 12

Deviled eggs have a place at the table during any Southern gathering. Whether it's Easter Sunday lunch or a Friday night cookout, deviled eggs are never a bad idea.

6   large hard-cooked eggs, peeled and rinsed
¼   cup mayonnaise
1½   teaspoons sweet pickle relish
1   teaspoon Dijon mustard
¼   teaspoon Slap Ya Mama Cajun Pepper Sauce
Paprika, pinch for each egg
Slap Ya Mama Hot Blend Cajun Seasoning, to taste
2   slices bacon, cooked and chopped

1. With a knife, carefully cut each egg in half lengthwise. Place egg yolks in a large bowl, and set egg whites aside. To yolks, add mayonnaise, relish, mustard, and Slap Ya Mama Cajun Pepper Sauce; mash with a fork until ingredients are smooth.
2. Fill each egg white half with yolk mixture. Top each with a pinch of paprika and a few sprinkles of Slap Ya Mama Hot Blend Cajun Seasoning. Top each with bacon.

OYSTERS THREE WAYS

Not an oyster fan, you say? You might change your mind after you try these three ways to prepare and enjoy them.

SPINACH & ANDOUILLE OYSTERS

MAKES 24

- 9 ounces fresh baby spinach
- 3 tablespoons unsalted butter, divided
- 1 cup chopped onion
- ¼ cup chopped celery
- ¼ pound fresh andouille sausage
- ½ teaspoon Slap Ya Mama Hot Blend Cajun Seasoning
- 3 cloves garlic, minced
- ½ cup dry white wine
- ½ teaspoon kosher salt
- ½ cup panko (Japanese bread crumbs)
- 24 fresh oysters on the half shell
- Slap Ya Mama Green Pepper Sauce, to serve

1. Preheat oven to broil. Position oven rack 6 inches from broiler. Line a large rimmed baking sheet with foil.
2. Bring a large Dutch oven of salted water to a boil. Add spinach; cook, stirring constantly, just until wilted, about 1 minute. Drain; press to remove excess moisture. Set aside.
3. In a medium skillet, melt 1 tablespoon butter over medium heat. Add onion and celery; cook until browned, about 3 minutes. Add sausage and Slap Ya Mama Hot Blend Cajun Seasoning; cook, stirring frequently, until browned and crumbly, about 15 minutes.
4. Add garlic; cook for 2 minutes. Add wine, and scrape any browned bits from bottom of pan. Continue cooking until wine reduces, about 30 seconds. Add spinach and salt; cook until liquid is almost evaporated, about 15 minutes. Remove from heat; stir in bread crumbs and remaining 2 tablespoons butter.
5. Arrange oysters on prepared pan. Top each oyster with about 1 tablespoon sausage mixture.
6. Broil until lightly browned, about 5 minutes. Serve with Slap Ya Mama Green Pepper Sauce.

BRIE & BACON OYSTERS

MAKES 16

- 3 slices bacon
- 1 tablespoon unsalted butter
- ¼ cup minced shallot
- 1 clove garlic, minced
- 2 tablespoons dry white wine
- 1 cup heavy whipping cream
- 1 (8-ounce) wheel of Brie, rind trimmed
- 4 ounces cream cheese, softened
- ¼ cup grated Parmesan cheese
- 1 teaspoon Slap Ya Mama Original Blend Cajun Seasoning
- 2 cups rock salt
- 16 fresh oysters on the half shell
- 2 cups panko (Japanese bread crumbs)

1. In a large saucepan, cook bacon over medium heat until crisp. Remove bacon, and let drain on paper towels, reserving 1 tablespoon drippings in pan.
2. Add butter to pan; stir in shallot and garlic, and cook until tender. Add wine, and cook until wine evaporates. Add cream, and bring to a simmer. Add Brie, cream cheese, and Parmesan, stirring until melted and combined. Stir in Slap Ya Mama Original Blend Cajun Seasoning. Cover and refrigerate until cold.
3. Preheat oven to 450°. Pour rock salt onto a rimmed baking sheet.
4. Arrange oysters on prepared pan. Top each oyster with about 2 tablespoons cheese sauce and 2 tablespoons bread crumbs.
5. Bake until browned and bubbly, 10 to 15 minutes. Crumble reserved bacon, and sprinkle over oysters.

NEW ORLEANS BARBECUE OYSTERS

MAKES 12

- 2 cups rock salt
- 3 tablespoons unsalted butter, divided
- 1 clove garlic, minced
- Juice of 1 lemon
- 3 tablespoons Worcestershire sauce
- 1 tablespoon Slap Ya Mama Cajun Hot Sauce
- 2 teaspoons Slap Ya Mama Hot Blend Cajun Seasoning
- 1 teaspoon ground black pepper
- ½ teaspoon kosher salt
- 1 cup amber beer
- 12 fresh oysters on the half shell
- Garnish: roughly chopped fresh rosemary

1. Preheat oven to broil. Pour rock salt onto a rimmed baking sheet.
2. In a small saucepan, melt 1 tablespoon butter over medium-high heat. Add garlic; cook until lightly browned, about 2 minutes. Add lemon juice, Worcestershire, Slap Ya Mama Cajun Hot Sauce, Slap Ya Mama Hot Blend Cajun Seasoning, pepper, and kosher salt; cook for 2 minutes. Add beer; cook until reduced by half, 15 to 20 minutes. Add remaining 2 tablespoons butter, stirring until combined.
3. Arrange oysters on prepared pan. Divide sauce among oysters.
4. Broil until edges of oysters are curled, 5 to 10 minutes. Garnish with rosemary, if desired.

CRAB CAKES

MAKES ABOUT 10

Simple to make and fry, these crab cakes are golden brown and prepared with Slap Ya Mama White Pepper Blend Seasoning. You'll be back for seconds!

½   cup plus 2 tablespoons olive oil, divided
6   green onions, chopped
1   (16-ounce) container crabmeat, picked free of shell and drained
8   ounces buttery round crackers, crushed
1   large egg
1   tablespoon mayonnaise
1   teaspoon dry mustard
1   teaspoon Slap Ya Mama White Pepper Blend Seasoning
1   cup panko (Japanese bread crumbs) or dry bread crumbs
Lemon wedges, to serve
Garnish: sliced green onion

1. In a large skillet, heat 2 tablespoons oil over high heat. Add green onion; cook briefly until tender. Let cool slightly.
2. In a large bowl, combine green onion, crabmeat, crushed crackers, egg, mayonnaise, mustard, and Slap Ya Mama White Pepper Blend Seasoning. Shape mixture into ½-inch-thick patties. Coat patties with bread crumbs.
3. In a large skillet, heat remaining ½ cup oil over medium-high heat. Cook patties until golden brown on both sides. Let drain briefly on paper towels, and serve hot with lemon wedges. Garnish with green onion, if desired.

STUFFED JALAPEÑOS WRAPPED IN BACON

MAKES 10

A party just isn't a party until someone whips up a batch of these stuffed jalapeños—and as an added bonus, there's bacon involved. Get ready for a spicy treat!

- 1 (8-ounce) package cream cheese, softened
- ¼ cup sun-dried tomatoes, diced
- 1⅓ tablespoons finely chopped fresh cilantro
- 3 cloves garlic, diced
- 1 teaspoon Slap Ya Mama Hot Blend Cajun Seasoning
- 10 fresh jalapeños
- 10 slices thick-cut bacon, lightly cooked
- 20 wooden picks, soaked in water for about 15 minutes

1. Preheat oven to 350°.
2. In a small bowl, combine cream cheese, sun-dried tomatoes, cilantro, garlic, and Slap Ya Mama Hot Blend Cajun Seasoning; set aside.
3. Place jalapeño on cutting board, and cut a lengthwise seam along side. Make a cross cut (about three-fourths of the way through the jalapeño) just below top of jalapeño, to create a T-shaped cut in jalapeño. Carefully open jalapeño, and with a small paring knife, carefully remove core and seeds, creating an empty shell. Rinse, and set aside. Repeat with all remaining jalapeños.
4. With a spoon, fill each jalapeño with cream cheese mixture. Be sure not to overfill; jalapeños should still be able to close up. Wrap each jalapeño with one slice lightly cooked bacon, securing it in place with about 2 wooden picks per jalapeño. Place jalapeños on a rimmed baking sheet with seams facing down.
5. Bake until bacon is crispy, about 45 minutes. Remove wooden picks just before serving. Serve immediately.

Note: To grill, cook over indirect heat, turning occasionally, until bacon is crispy.

MAMA JEN'S SHRIMP DIP AND CRAB DIP

A good party snack should be irresistible and addictive, and these two favorite seafood dips are just that. You'll never have to ask, "What can I bring?" again.

MAMA JEN'S SHRIMP DIP
MAKES 8 SERVINGS

- 1 (8-ounce) package cream cheese, softened
- 6 tablespoons mayonnaise
- ¼ cup ketchup
- ¼ cup chopped onion
- ¼ cup chopped bell pepper
- 1 (4-ounce) can tiny shrimp, drained
- Slap Ya Mama White Pepper Blend Seasoning, to taste
- Bagel chips, to serve

1. In a small bowl, stir together cream cheese and mayonnaise. Add ketchup, onion, and bell pepper. Stir in shrimp and Slap Ya Mama White Pepper Blend Seasoning. Refrigerate for 1 hour before serving. Serve with bagel chips.

CRAB DIP
MAKES 12 SERVINGS

- 1 (8-ounce) package cream cheese, softened
- ½ cup mayonnaise
- ⅓ cup shredded Swiss cheese
- ¼ cup minced shallot
- 1 tablespoon fresh lemon juice
- 2 teaspoons Slap Ya Mama Cajun Hot Sauce
- 2 teaspoons Worcestershire sauce
- 2 teaspoons Slap Ya Mama Original Blend Cajun Seasoning
- ½ teaspoon dry mustard
- 1 tablespoon olive oil
- ¼ cup finely chopped yellow or red bell pepper
- 1 (8-ounce) container jumbo lump crabmeat, drained and picked free of shell
- 1 tablespoon minced garlic
- 2 tablespoons bourbon
- ½ cup shredded Parmesan cheese
- Garnish: sliced green onion
- Pita chips, to serve

1. Preheat oven to 325°. Spray a 1-quart baking dish with cooking spray.
2. In a large bowl, combine cream cheese, mayonnaise, Swiss, shallot, lemon juice, Slap Ya Mama Cajun Hot Sauce, Worcestershire, Slap Ya Mama Original Blend Cajun Seasoning, and mustard.
3. In a medium skillet, heat oil over medium-high heat. Add bell pepper; cook, stirring frequently, until tender, 2 to 3 minutes. Add crabmeat and garlic; cook for 1 minute. Add bourbon; cook until liquid is reduced, about 2 minutes.
4. Fold crabmeat mixture into cream cheese mixture. Transfer to prepared pan. Sprinkle with Parmesan.
5. Bake until mixture is hot and bubbly and cheese is light golden brown, about 25 minutes. Let cool for 10 minutes. Garnish with green onion, if desired. Serve with pita chips.

PAW PAW DUB'S HOT DIP

MAKES 8 SERVINGS

Named after its biggest fan, Paw Paw Dub, you'll fall in love with this cheesy, spicy dip that will have everyone asking for the recipe!

1 cup mayonnaise
5 tablespoons margarine, softened
2 cups shredded Cheddar Jack cheese
½ onion, chopped
½ green bell pepper, chopped
⅓ cup chopped fresh jalapeño
Slap Ya Mama Hot Blend Cajun Seasoning, to taste
Assorted crackers and chips, to serve

1. In a small bowl, stir together mayonnaise and margarine until smooth. Add cheese, onion, bell pepper, jalapeño, and Slap Ya Mama Hot Blend Cajun Seasoning. Refrigerate for at least 1 hour. Serve with crackers and chips.

COOKING TIP FROM MAMA JEN

Before you start cooking, be sure to have all of your ingredients right in front of you. Open any cans, chop your vegetables, and have water on hand, if needed, to add to your sauce.

CRAWFISH BREAD BOWL DIP

MAKES 20 SERVINGS

What could possibly make a cheesy dip filled with savory vegetables and crawfish better? Aunt Celeste knows—serving it inside a bread bowl, of course.

- ½ cup unsalted butter
- 1 medium yellow onion, chopped
- ½ red bell pepper, chopped
- ½ green bell pepper, chopped
- 2 cloves garlic, minced
- 1 tablespoon Worcestershire sauce
- 4 ounces cream cheese
- 1 (10.5-ounce) can cream of shrimp soup
- 1 (8-ounce) can tomato sauce
- 1 (5.5-ounce) can vegetable juice
- ½ cup shredded Monterey Jack cheese
- ½ cup half-and-half
- 1 pound cooked crawfish tails with fat
- 2 teaspoons lemon zest
- Slap Ya Mama Original Blend Cajun Seasoning, to taste
- Handful chopped green onion
- 3 tablespoons chopped fresh parsley
- 1 teaspoon dried thyme
- Dash Slap Ya Mama Cajun Hot Sauce or Slap Ya Mama Green Pepper Sauce
- 1 (16-ounce) round loaf Hawaiian sweet bread
- Garnish: chopped fresh parsley
- Assorted crackers, to serve

1. Preheat oven to 325°.

2. In a medium saucepan, melt butter over medium heat. Add onion, bell peppers, and garlic; cook until tender. Stir in Worcestershire. Add cream cheese, stirring until melted. Add soup, tomato sauce, and vegetable juice, stirring until well combined. Cook, stirring frequently, for 15 minutes. Add cheese and half-and-half, stirring until cheese is melted.

3. Season crawfish with lemon zest and Slap Ya Mama Original Blend Cajun Seasoning. Add crawfish mixture, green onion, parsley, thyme, and Slap Ya Mama Cajun Hot Sauce to pan. Cook over low heat until thickened, about 3 minutes. (Thicken with flour, if necessary.) Remove from heat.

4. Cut top off bread round, and set aside. Hollow out inside of loaf. Make sure enough bread is left inside so that bread does not have any holes. Press bread down inside bowl. Leftover bread can be cubed and baked for dipping in crawfish dip.

5. Place bread bowl on a baking sheet. Pour crawfish mixture into bread bowl.

6. Bake for 30 minutes. Return top of bread round to bread bowl, and cover entire round with foil. Bake for 30 minutes more. Remove top of bread round, and garnish with parsley, if desired. Serve warm with bread pieces and crackers.

CRAWFISH HAND PIES AND CAJUN MEAT PIES

Whether you're serving seafood lovers or meat eaters, these two different styles of hand pies are packed full of flavorful ingredients that will make everyone happy.

CRAWFISH HAND PIES
MAKES 8 SERVINGS

- 1 large egg, lightly beaten
- 1 teaspoon water
- 3 tablespoons unsalted butter, melted
- 1 tablespoon Slap Ya Mama Original Blend Cajun Seasoning
- 1 (14-ounce) package empanada dough*
- 2 cups Quick Crawfish Étouffée (recipe follows)

Cajun Mayonnaise (recipe follows)

1. Preheat oven to 350°. Line a rimmed baking sheet with parchment paper.
2. In a small bowl, whisk together egg and 1 teaspoon water until combined. In another small bowl, stir together melted butter and Cajun seasoning.
3. On a lightly floured surface, roll each empanada dough round to make it about ½ inch larger. Spoon about 2 tablespoons Quick Crawfish Étouffée onto center of each dough round. Brush edges of dough with egg wash. Fold dough over filling, pressing firmly to seal. Crimp edges with a fork, if desired. Place on prepared pan. Brush with butter mixture.
4. Bake until golden, about 30 minutes. Serve with Cajun Mayonnaise.

*We used Goya Empanada Dough.

QUICK CRAWFISH ÉTOUFFÉE

- ¼ cup unsalted butter
- ½ cup chopped sweet onion
- ½ cup chopped celery
- ½ cup chopped red bell pepper
- 2 cloves garlic, minced
- 3 tablespoons all-purpose flour
- ½ cup dry sherry
- 1 cup seafood stock
- 2 tablespoons extra-concentrated tomato paste
- 2 tablespoons Slap Ya Mama Cajun Hot Sauce
- 2 bay leaves
- 1 teaspoon kosher salt
- ½ teaspoon ground black pepper
- 1 pound cooked crawfish tails

1. In a large skillet, melt butter over medium-high heat. Add onion, celery, and bell pepper; cook until tender, about 10 minutes. Add garlic; cook until tender, about 1 minute. Add flour; cook, stirring constantly, until combined, about 2 minutes. Stir in sherry; cook until reduced by half, about 3 minutes. Add stock, tomato paste, Slap Ya Mama Cajun Hot Sauce, bay leaves, salt, and black pepper. Bring to a boil, and cook until mixture begins to thicken. Add crawfish; reduce heat, and simmer for about 8 minutes.

CAJUN MAYONNAISE

- ¼ cup mayonnaise
- 1 tablespoon Slap Ya Mama Original Blend Cajun Seasoning
- 1 tablespoon Slap Ya Mama Cajun Hot Sauce
- 2 teaspoons red wine vinegar

1. In a small bowl, combine mayonnaise, Slap Ya Mama Original Blend Cajun Seasoning, Slap Ya Mama Cajun Hot Sauce, and vinegar. Cover and refrigerate until ready to serve.

CAJUN MEAT PIES

MAKES 8 SERVINGS

- 1 pound sweet potatoes
- ¼ pound andouille sausage, casings removed
- ¾ pound ground beef
- ¼ pound ground pork
- 2½ tablespoons unsalted butter, divided
- ½ cup plus ⅓ cup finely chopped onion, divided
- ⅓ cup finely chopped celery
- ⅓ cup finely chopped green bell pepper
- 1½ tablespoons Slap Ya Mama Original Blend Cajun Seasoning, divided
- ½ tablespoon Worcestershire sauce
- 2 teaspoons minced garlic
- 1 teaspoon Slap Ya Mama Cajun Hot Sauce
- ¾ cup finely chopped carrot
- 1 teaspoon kosher salt
- 1 teaspoon ground black pepper
- 2 (8-ounce) packages frozen pastry shells, thawed

1. Preheat oven to 400°.
2. On a rimmed baking sheet, place sweet potatoes.
3. Bake until softened, about 1 hour. Remove from oven. Increase oven temperature to broil.
4. In the work bowl of a food processor, place andouille sausage; pulse until finely ground. In a large bowl, combine sausage, beef, and pork.
5. Heat a large Dutch oven over medium heat. Add meat mixture; cook, stirring and breaking up meat with a wooden spoon, until browned. Remove meat using a slotted spoon, and place in a large bowl. Reserve drippings in a small bowl.
6. Add 1 tablespoon butter to Dutch oven, and melt over medium-high heat. Add ⅓ cup onion, celery, bell pepper, 1 tablespoon Slap Ya Mama Original Blend Cajun Seasoning, Worcestershire, garlic, and Slap Ya Mama Cajun Hot Sauce; cook, stirring and scraping bottom of pan with a wooden spoon, until vegetables are tender, about 5 minutes. Remove onion mixture, and place in a medium bowl.
7. To Dutch oven, add reserved drippings, carrot, salt, black pepper, remaining ½ cup onion, and remaining ½ tablespoon Slap Ya Mama Original Blend Cajun Seasoning; cook over medium heat, stirring frequently, until carrot is tender. Transfer to bowl with onion mixture.
8. Scoop out sweet potato flesh into a large bowl. Add salt and black pepper to taste and remaining 1½ tablespoons butter. Using a potato masher, mash until smooth.
9. Arrange pastry shells on rimmed baking sheets. To each shell, add 1 heaping tablespoon beef mixture and 1 tablespoon onion mixture. Spoon mashed sweet potato on top.
10. Broil until crust is browned, 1 to 2 minutes. Let cool slightly.

BLOODY MARY PICKLED SHRIMP

MAKES 8 SERVINGS

Bright, zesty, and just a little spicy, this recipe marinates boiled shrimp in our signature Slap Ya Mama Bloody Mary Mix with fresh vegetables for the perfect party snack or afternoon treat.

6	cups water
2	pounds jumbo fresh shrimp, peeled and deveined (tails left on)
2	cups Slap Ya Mama Bloody Mary Mix
1	(14-ounce) can halved artichoke hearts, drained
1	cup thinly sliced red onion
½	cup chopped celery
½	cup thinly sliced red bell pepper
½	cup thinly sliced yellow bell pepper
1	lime, sliced
4	bay leaves
3	large fresh thyme sprigs
3	tablespoons vegetable oil
1	tablespoon Slap Ya Mama Signature Blend Chili Lime Seasoning

Garnish: lime wedges
Sliced French bread, toasted, to serve

1. In a large saucepan, bring 6 cups water to a boil. Add shrimp. Cook just until shrimp are pink and firm, about 1½ to 2 minutes. (Do not overcook.) Drain. Transfer to an ice water bath to stop the cooking process. Drain.

2. In a large glass bowl, stir together shrimp, Slap Ya Mama Bloody Mary Mix, artichokes, red onion, celery, bell peppers, lime slices, bay leaves, thyme sprigs, vegetable oil, and Slap Ya Mama Signature Blend Chili Lime Seasoning. Cover and refrigerate for 24 hours, stirring occasionally. Discard bay leaves and thyme sprigs. Garnish with lime wedges, if desired. Serve with toasted French bread.

BUFFALO CHICKEN WINGS

MAKES 4 TO 6 SERVINGS

Spicy, sweet, and just a bit tangy—these chicken wings have it all.

- 5 pounds chicken wings
- 1 cup mayonnaise
- ½ cup plus 2 tablespoons Slap Ya Mama Buffalo Wing Sauce, divided
- ¼ cup honey
- 1 tablespoon lime zest
- 2 tablespoons fresh lime juice

Celery sticks and Slap Ya Mama Buffalo Wing Sauce, to serve

1. Cut off and discard wing tips; cut wings in half at joint, if desired. Place in a large resealable plastic bag.
2. In a small bowl, stir together mayonnaise, 2 tablespoons Slap Ya Mama Buffalo Wing Sauce, honey, and lime zest and juice. Pour over wings, tossing to coat. Seal bag, and refrigerate for at least 4 hours or up to overnight.
3. Preheat oven to 400°. Line a large rimmed baking sheet with foil; place wire rack on foil. Drain wings, discarding marinade. Place in a single layer on prepared pan.
4. Bake until golden brown, 45 to 50 minutes, turning wings every 10 minutes to prevent burning.
5. Drizzle remaining ½ cup Slap Ya Mama Buffalo Wing Sauce over wings. Serve immediately with celery sticks and additional Slap Ya Mama Buffalo Wing Sauce.

Kitchen Tip: You can also toss the wings in Slap Ya Mama Buffalo Wing Sauce and serve.

GRATTONS

MAKES ABOUT 2 CUPS

Also known as cracklin's, these crunchy bites of fried pork belly are generously coated in Slap Ya Mama Original Blend Cajun Seasoning for even more flavor.

1   pound skin-on pork belly
4   cups lard or vegetable oil
Slap Ya Mama Original Blend Cajun Seasoning
Slap Ya Mama Cajun Pepper Sauce, to serve

1. On a cutting board, trim a thin layer of pork from bottom side of pork belly. Reserve for another use. Turn pork belly skin side up, and cut into 1-inch pieces.
2. In a large cast-iron Dutch oven, heat lard or oil over medium-high heat until a deep-fry thermometer registers 250°. Add pork belly, stirring gently to prevent pieces from sticking together. (Adjust heat as necessary to maintain an oil temperature of 200° to 250°.) Cook, stirring frequently, until skin is blistered and golden brown, about 25 minutes. Remove pork belly using a slotted spoon, and let drain on a paper towel-lined baking sheet. Let cool slightly, about 10 minutes. Refrigerate until cold, about 1 hour.
3. In the same pan, reheat lard or oil over medium-high heat until a deep-fry thermometer registers 375°. Fry refrigerated pork belly in batches until golden brown, about 2 minutes. Remove pork belly using a slotted spoon, and let drain on a paper towel-lined baking sheet. Immediately sprinkle with Slap Ya Mama Original Blend Cajun Seasoning, tossing to coat. Serve with Slap Ya Mama Cajun Pepper Sauce.

SWEET POTATO CHEESE FRIES WITH DEBRIS

MAKES ABOUT 4 SERVINGS

We loaded sweet potato waffle fries with our Cajun seasoning, sharp white cheese, and savory debris for your new favorite game-day snack.

1   (20-ounce) bag frozen waffle-cut sweet potato fries
1   (8-ounce) block sharp white Cheddar cheese, crumbled
1   teaspoon Slap Ya Mama Hot Blend Cajun Seasoning
2   cups roast beef debris (see note below), heated
¼   cup chopped green onion
Garnish: Slap Ya Mama Hot Blend Cajun Seasoning, Slap Ya Mama Cajun Hot Sauce

1. Preheat oven to 400°. Line a rimmed baking sheet with foil.
2. Prepare sweet potato fries according to oven package directions on prepared pan. Top fries with Cheddar and Slap Ya Mama Hot Blend Cajun Seasoning.
3. Bake until cheese is melted, 6 to 8 minutes. Spoon roast beef debris onto fries. Sprinkle with green onion. Garnish with Slap Ya Mama Hot Blend Cajun Seasoning and Slap Ya Mama Cajun Hot Sauce, if desired.

Note: We used the recipe for debris from our Debris Po' Boys on page 115.

BOUDIN ROLLS WITH SPICY CANE SYRUP

MAKES 12

A sweet favorite gets a savory twist with a swirl of cheese and boudin. Then, the rolls are topped with a Spicy Cane Syrup for a final, delicious touch.

DOUGH:
- ¾ cup whole milk
- ½ cup water
- ⅓ cup unsalted butter, cubed
- 4 to 4¼ cups all-purpose flour, divided, plus more for dusting
- 2 tablespoons sugar
- 1 tablespoon kosher salt
- 1 (0.25-ounce) package active dry yeast
- 1 large egg, room temperature

FILLING:
- 1 (8-ounce) package cream cheese, softened
- 1 cup freshly grated Parmesan cheese
- ½ cup sliced green onion
- 2 teaspoons Slap Ya Mama Original Blend Cajun Seasoning
- 3 cups boudin sausage

2 tablespoons unsalted butter, melted
Spicy Cane Syrup (recipe follows), to serve

1. For dough: In a medium saucepan, heat milk and ½ cup water over medium heat until scalding. Remove from heat. Add butter; let stand, stirring occasionally, until butter is melted and an instant-read thermometer registers 120° to 130°.

2. In the bowl of a stand mixer, whisk together 2 cups flour, sugar, salt, and yeast by hand. Add warm milk mixture; using the paddle attachment, beat at low speed until combined. Add egg, beating until combined. With mixer on low speed, gradually add 2 cups flour, beating just until a shaggy dough comes together and stopping to scrape sides of bowl.

3. Switch to the dough hook attachment. Beat at low speed until a soft, somewhat sticky dough forms, about 20 minutes, stopping to scrape sides of bowl and dough hook; add up to remaining ¼ cup flour, 1 tablespoon at a time, if dough is too sticky. Beat until a smooth, elastic dough forms, 3 to 5 minutes. Turn out dough onto a clean surface, and shape into a smooth round.

4. Lightly oil a large bowl. Place dough in bowl, turning to grease top. Cover and let rise in a warm, draft-free place until doubled in size, about 1 hour.

5. For filling: In a large bowl, stir together cream cheese, Parmesan, green onion, and Slap Ya Mama Original Blend Cajun Seasoning until smooth. Fold in boudin until just combined.

6. Spray a 13x9-inch baking pan with cooking spray.

7. Lightly punch down dough. Cover and let stand for 10 minutes. Turn out dough onto a very lightly floured surface, and roll into an 18x12-inch rectangle. Using a small offset spatula, spread boudin mixture onto dough, leaving a ½-inch border on one long side. Starting with one long side, roll dough into a log; pinch seam to seal. Using a serrated knife dipped in flour, cut log into 12 slices (about 1½ inches thick each). Place slices, cut side down, in prepared pan. Cover with plastic wrap, and let rise in a warm, draft-free place until dough fills pan, about 30 minutes.

8. Preheat oven to 350°.

9. Bake until golden brown, 35 to 40 minutes. Brush with melted butter. Drizzle with Spicy Cane Syrup.

SPICY CANE SYRUP

MAKES ½ CUP

- ½ cup cane syrup
- 1 tablespoon crushed red pepper
- 2 teaspoons Slap Ya Mama Original Blend Cajun seasoning
- 1 tablespoon cane vinegar

1. In a small saucepan, combine cane syrup, red pepper, and Slap Ya Mama Original Blend Cajun Seasoning. Heat over medium-low heat until gently simmering; remove from heat. Let stand for 15 minutes. Stir in vinegar. Let cool completely.

GREEN TOMATO SALSA

MAKES 2 CUPS

No party is complete without chips and salsa. Skip the store-bought salsa and make your own with this easy recipe.

- 1½ cups chopped green tomato
- ¼ cup minced seeded jalapeño
- 2 tablespoons fresh lime juice
- 1 tablespoon chopped fresh cilantro
- 1 teaspoon minced garlic
- 1 teaspoon Slap Ya Mama Signature Blend Chili Lime Seasoning
- ½ teaspoon Slap Ya Mama Original Blend Cajun Seasoning

1. In a medium bowl, stir together all ingredients. Cover and refrigerate up to 1 week.

SAVORY SWEET POTATO HAND PIES
MAKES 20

Dipped in a creamy sauce, these delicious hand pies are approved by kids of all ages.

2	pounds sweet potato, peeled and cut into ½-inch cubes
¾	teaspoon Slap Ya Mama Original Blend Cajun Seasoning, plus more to garnish
½	teaspoon kosher salt
¼	teaspoon ground black pepper
¼	teaspoon ground cumin
1	tablespoon vegetable oil, plus more for frying
½	cup minced red onion
½	medium jalapeño, seeded and finely chopped
1¼	teaspoon grated fresh ginger
¾	cup drained rinsed canned black beans
1	tablespoon chopped fresh cilantro
	Pie Dough (recipe follows)
1	large egg
2	tablespoons water
	Sour Cream-Lime Sauce (recipe follows)

1. Preheat oven to 425°. Line a large rimmed baking sheet with foil. Spray with cooking spray.
2. In a large bowl, combine sweet potato, Slap Ya Mama Original Blend Cajun Seasoning, salt, black pepper, and cumin. Spread sweet potato mixture onto prepared pan.
3. Bake, turning occasionally, until tender, 20 to 25 minutes.
4. In a medium saucepan, heat 1 tablespoon oil over medium heat. Add onion; cook until tender, about 2 minutes. Add jalapeño and ginger; cook until jalapeño is tender. Remove from heat, and stir in sweet potato mixture, black beans, and cilantro. Let cool completely.
5. Cut Pie Dough into 20 pieces. On a lightly floured surface, roll each piece of dough into a 5½-inch circle, and place on a parchment-lined baking sheet. Refrigerate for 10 minutes. Using a 5-inch round cutter, cut rounds from each piece of dough. In a small bowl, whisk together egg and 2 tablespoons water.
6. Place about 3 tablespoons filling in center of each round, and press seams to seal. Using a fork, crimp along edges of pie. Using a pastry wheel, cut along edges to further seal. Freeze pies 10 minutes before frying.
7. In a large Dutch oven, pour oil to a depth of 4 inches, and heat over medium heat until a deep-fry thermometer registers 365°. Line a rimmed baking sheet with paper towels, and place a wire rack on top.
8. Using a slotted spoon, gently place pies, 4 to 5 at a time, in hot oil. Fry until golden brown, about 2 minutes per side. Remove from oil, and let drain on prepared pan. Garnish with Slap Ya Mama Original Blend Cajun Seasoning. Serve with Sour Cream-Lime Sauce.

PIE DOUGH
MAKES DOUGH FOR 20 HAND PIES

5¾	cups all-purpose flour
2½	teaspoons kosher salt
1¼	teaspoons baking powder
¾	cup cold lard
2	large eggs
1½	cups whole milk

1. In a large bowl, whisk together flour, salt, and baking powder. Using a pastry blender or 2 forks, cut in lard until mixture is crumbly.
2. In a small bowl, whisk together eggs and milk. Pour egg mixture over flour mixture, and lightly toss with your hands until a dough starts to form. Knead together 4 to 5 times, and let rest for 10 minutes. Cover and refrigerate for 2 hours before using.

SOUR CREAM-LIME SAUCE
MAKES ABOUT 1⅓ CUPS

1	cup sour cream
3	tablespoons fresh lime juice
2	tablespoons mayonnaise
2	tablespoons chopped fresh cilantro
¼	teaspoon Slap Ya Mama Original Blend Cajun Seasoning, plus more to garnish

1. In a small bowl, whisk together all ingredients. Serve immediately. Garnish with Slap Ya Mama Original Blend Cajun Seasoning, if desired.

CHAPTER THREE
SOUPS & SALADS

Every course is hearty and filling in Cajun Country

SEAFOOD GUMBO

MAKES 6 TO 8 SERVINGS

Nothing feeds the belly and the soul like a warm bowl of gumbo. Served over rice, this dish combines all your seafood favorites in one comforting bowl.

- 1 cup vegetable oil
- 1 cup all-purpose flour
- 3 cups chopped fresh okra
- 1½ cups chopped onion
- 1 cup chopped green bell pepper
- 1 cup chopped red bell pepper
- 1 cup chopped celery
- 3 tablespoons minced garlic
- 6 cups seafood stock
- 1 (8-ounce) container crab claw meat, picked free of shell
- 1½ cups amber beer
- 2 tablespoons filé powder
- 1 tablespoon Worcestershire sauce
- 2 teaspoons kosher salt
- 2 teaspoons Slap Ya Mama Original Blend Cajun Seasoning
- 1 teaspoon Slap Ya Mama Hot Blend Cajun Seasoning
- 2 bay leaves
- 1 pound medium fresh shrimp, peeled and deveined
- 1 pound red snapper fillets, chopped
- 2 (8-ounce) containers shucked oysters, drained
- 1 (8-ounce) container jumbo lump crabmeat, picked free of shell
- ¼ cup chopped fresh parsley
- Hot cooked rice, to serve
- Garnish: sliced green onion

1. In an 8-quart stockpot, heat oil over medium heat for about 5 minutes; add flour, stirring to combine. Cook, stirring frequently, until a peanut butter-colored roux forms, about 20 minutes.

2. Add okra, onion, bell peppers, celery, and garlic; cook, stirring frequently, for 5 minutes. Add stock, crab claw meat, beer, filé powder, Worcestershire, salt, Slap Ya Mama Original Blend Cajun Seasoning, Slap Ya Mama Hot Blend Cajun Seasoning, and bay leaves; bring to a boil. Reduce heat to medium, and simmer for about 1 hour.

3. Add shrimp, fish, oysters, and lump crabmeat; cook until seafood is cooked through, 8 to 10 minutes. Stir in parsley. Serve over hot cooked rice. Garnish with green onion, if desired.

COOKING TIP FROM MAMA JEN

When the first cool snap arrives, cook a gumbo. It's always better the next day.

SHRIMP & CORN SOUP WITH TASSO

MAKES 8 SERVINGS

Tasso adds an extra kick to this flavor-packed and perfectly creamy soup.

- 2 tablespoons olive oil
- 2 cups chopped tasso or cooked ham
- 1 large onion, chopped
- 1 medium bell pepper, chopped
- 2 cloves garlic, minced
- 1½ tablespoons Slap Ya Mama Original Blend Cajun Seasoning, divided
- 1 (8-ounce) package cream cheese
- 2 (14-ounce) cans cream-style corn
- 1 (14-ounce) can diced tomatoes
- 1 (10-ounce) can cream of shrimp soup
- 1 (10-ounce) can cream of mushroom soup
- 2 cups whole milk
- ¾ cup water
- 1 pound medium fresh shrimp, peeled and deveined
- 2 tablespoons chopped fresh parsley
- Garnish: chopped green onion

1. In a Dutch oven, heat oil over medium heat. Add tasso, onion, bell pepper, garlic, and 1 tablespoon Slap Ya Mama Original Blend Cajun Seasoning; cook until onion is translucent. Stir in cream cheese, and cook until softened. Add corn, tomatoes, soups, milk, and remaining ½ tablespoon Slap Ya Mama Original Blend Cajun Seasoning; cook, stirring constantly, for 8 to 10 minutes. Add ¾ cup water; increase heat, and bring to a light boil. Add shrimp, and return to a light boil. Reduce heat, and simmer for 10 minutes. Stir in parsley, and simmer for 5 minutes. Garnish with green onion, if desired.

COOKING TIP FROM MAMA JEN

Always make sure you can see in the pot — if not, get a stool!

TURTLE SOUP

MAKES 8 SERVINGS

This dish is essential to the full experience of Louisiana cuisine and is always served with sherry.

- 1 pound boneless turtle meat
- 2 tablespoons olive oil
- 2 green bell peppers, diced
- 2 onions, diced
- 1 stalk celery, diced
- 6 cloves garlic, minced
- 2 tablespoons paprika
- 2 bay leaves
- 2 teaspoons Slap Ya Mama Low Sodium Cajun Seasoning
- 2 teaspoons dried thyme
- 1½ teaspoons dried oregano
- 1 teaspoon Slap Ya Mama Hot Blend Cajun Seasoning
- 1 teaspoon ground cumin
- 1 teaspoon ground coriander
- 1 teaspoon chili powder
- Dark Flour (recipe follows)
- 8 cups chicken broth, divided
- 1 (28-ounce) can crushed tomatoes
- 2 cups dry sherry
- 1 cup dry red wine
- 3 hard-cooked eggs, peeled and cubed
- ½ cup chopped fresh parsley
- ½ cup fresh lemon juice
- Salt and ground black pepper, to taste
- Garnish: chopped fresh parsley, lemon slices
- Dry sherry and French bread, to serve

1. Trim fat and gristle from turtle meat. Cut meat into 1-inch cubes, and grind in a meat grinder.

2. In a large Dutch oven, heat oil over medium-high heat. Add turtle meat, bell pepper, onion, celery, and garlic; cook until turtle is browned and onion is tender, 6 to 8 minutes. Stir in paprika, bay leaves, Slap Ya Mama Low Sodium Cajun Seasoning, thyme, oregano, Slap Ya Mama Hot Blend Cajun Seasoning, cumin, coriander, and chili powder; cook for 2 minutes.

3. In a medium bowl, stir together Dark Flour and 2 cups broth until smooth; stir into turtle mixture. Gradually stir in tomatoes, sherry, wine, and the remaining 6 cups broth; bring to a boil. Reduce heat; cover and simmer, stirring occasionally, for 45 minutes. Remove bay leaves.

4. Add eggs, parsley, and lemon juice; cook for 15 minutes. Season to taste with salt and black pepper. Divide soup among serving bowls. Garnish with parsley and lemon slices, if desired. Serve with sherry and French bread.

DARK FLOUR
MAKES 2 CUPS

- 2 cups all-purpose flour

1. Preheat oven to 350°.

2. Spread flour onto a rimmed baking sheet.

3. Bake until dark brown and nutty, stirring occasionally at first and frequently as flour begins to darken. Let cool completely before using, and store in an airtight container for up to 1 month.

FRIED OYSTER SALAD

MAKES 24

Oysters on the half shell are deep-fried to perfection and served over a creamy spinach mixture. Get 'em while they're hot!

2	(6-ounce) bags fresh baby spinach
2	tablespoons canola oil
2	cloves garlic, minced
2	tablespoons heavy whipping cream
2	teaspoons anise-flavored liqueur
1	teaspoon Slap Ya Mama Cajun Pepper Sauce
4	cups plus 1¾ teaspoons kosher salt, divided
½	teaspoon ground black pepper, divided
24	fresh oysters on the half shell
1½	cups lightly packed grated Parmesan cheese
¾	cup panko (Japanese bread crumbs)
1½	cups whole buttermilk
2	cups yellow cornmeal
¼	cup all-purpose flour
½	teaspoon Slap Ya Mama Hot Blend Cajun Seasoning

Vegetable oil, for frying
Garnish: Slap Ya Mama Cajun Pepper Sauce
Lemon wedges, to serve

1. In the work bowl of a food processor, pulse spinach in batches until finely chopped.
2. In a large skillet, heat canola oil over medium-high heat. Add garlic; cook until lightly browned, about 1 minute. Gradually add spinach; cook until wilted, about 5 minutes. Remove from heat. Stir in cream, liqueur, Slap Ya Mama Cajun Pepper Sauce, ¼ teaspoon salt, and ¼ teaspoon pepper.
3. Preheat oven to 400°.
4. Remove oysters from shells, reserving oysters. On a rimmed baking sheet, place 4 cups salt. Arrange oyster shells on prepared pan. Fill shells with spinach mixture. Top with cheese and bread crumbs.
5. Bake until lightly browned, 8 to 10 minutes.
6. In a shallow dish, place buttermilk. In another shallow dish, whisk together cornmeal, flour, Slap Ya Mama Hot Blend Cajun Seasoning, remaining 1½ teaspoons salt, and remaining ¼ teaspoon pepper.
7. In a Dutch oven, pour vegetable oil to a depth of 2 inches, and heat over medium-high heat until a deep-fry thermometer registers 360°.
8. Dip oysters in buttermilk, letting excess drip off. Dredge oysters in cornmeal mixture, shaking off excess. Working in batches, carefully place oysters in hot oil. Fry until golden brown, 2 to 3 minutes. Let drain on paper towels. Place on top of spinach mixture. Garnish with Slap Ya Mama Cajun Pepper Sauce, if desired. Serve immediately with lemon wedges.

LAISSEZ LES BONS TEMPS ROULER!
THE REAL CAJUN MARDI GRAS
Let the Good Times Roll!

Mardi Gras—or Carnival—is celebrated in cities worldwide with strong Catholic ties. Although legend tells of French explorers Pierre Le Moyne d'Iberville and Sieur de Bienville hosting America's first Mardi Gras celebration near present-day New Orleans in 1699, historical record says it was first celebrated in the 1700s in present-day Mobile, Alabama, the capital of the French Louisiana territory. Today, communities along the Gulf Coast from Texas to Florida celebrate Mardi Gras season. Each area prides itself on its own unique customs, from parades, costumes, and formal balls to special food and libations.

Mardi Gras season begins on January 6, called the Epiphany or Twelfth Night, the day the three kings reached baby Jesus in Bethlehem. To mark the occasion, local bakeries make an oval-shaped pastry called a king cake. Inside each king cake is a small plastic baby that signifies the baby Jesus. The person who finds the baby in their cake slice has to host the next Mardi Gras party and provide the king cake. The Carnival season culminates on Fat Tuesday ("Mardi Gras" in French), the day before Ash Wednesday and Christian Lent. On Fat Tuesday and the weeks leading up to it, Catholics—and many Protestants—eat and drink whatever they wish before giving up meat on Fridays and other luxuries during the Lenten season of sacrifice and repentance.

Just 10 miles from Ville Platte is the small town of Mamou (pronounced Mah-moo), which hosts one of the most traditional Cajun Mardi Gras celebrations in the United States. The *Courir de Mardi Gras* (Fat Tuesday run) dates back to the *fête de la quémande* (feast of begging) of medieval France. Mamou revelers on horseback go door to door begging for ingredients to make a communal pot of gumbo. Dressed in simple costumes made of colorful scraps of fabric and donning a mask and *capuchon* (cone-shaped hat), men sing ballads in French. One home might provide a bell pepper, while another provides an onion or celery stalk or even a live chicken.

"The *capitaine* leads close to 200 men on horseback, and they dance on their horses," says Jennifer. "They get permission to go on the farmers' land to chase their chickens. The captured chickens are used in the gumbo. Behind them are trailers of men, women, and children playing music and throwing loot to the crowd, everyone having a good time."

Afterward, the fun goes on at Fred's Lounge, a famous Cajun French music joint in Mamou that opens every Saturday morning for the locals to dance. "Fred's Lounge is the first bar I ever went to in my life," says Jack. "I think Joe and I were 8 and 10 years old, maybe younger. But it was just so cold, and that was the only place we could go."

After the Mardi Gras fun, the Walkers invite their friends back to their Ville Platte house to warm up over a big pot of chicken and sausage gumbo—the true Cajun way of making gumbo, without tomatoes, okra, or seafood.

"New Orleans does things on a much grander scale with elaborate floats and balls," says Jack. "But Cajuns are more simplistic. We do the traditional Mardi Gras here. It's a big to-do because of all the people who get together."

CHICKEN & SAUSAGE GUMBO

MAKES 8 SERVINGS

This traditional gumbo is served by the Walker family after every Mardi Gras celebration.

1	cup vegetable oil
1	cup all-purpose flour
1	pound smoked pork sausage, cut into ½-inch pieces
1	onion, chopped
1	bell pepper, chopped
1	clove garlic, minced
2½	tablespoons Slap Ya Mama Original Blend Cajun Seasoning, divided
1	whole chicken, cut up and skin removed
1	bunch fresh parsley, chopped
1	bunch green onion, chopped

Hot cooked rice and Slap Ya Mama Cajun Pepper Sauce, to serve

1. In an 8-quart stockpot, heat oil over medium heat for 5 minutes; add flour, stirring to combine. Cook, stirring frequently, until a peanut butter-colored roux forms, about 20 minutes.

2. Fill a 10- to 12-quart stockpot halfway full with water, and bring to a boil over high heat. Add roux; boil, stirring occasionally, until roux is completely dissolved. Reduce heat to medium; add sausage, onion, bell pepper, garlic, and 2 tablespoons Slap Ya Mama Original Blend Cajun Seasoning. Boil for 15 minutes.

3. Season chicken with remaining ½ tablespoon Slap Ya Mama Original Blend Cajun Seasoning, and add to pot. Add water to pot until it is almost full. Bring to a boil, and boil for 50 minutes.

4. Reduce heat to low, and add parsley and green onion; cook for 10 minutes. Serve over hot cooked rice, and add a few dashes Slap Ya Mama Cajun Pepper Sauce.

SUMMER OKRA & TOMATO SALAD

MAKES 6 SERVINGS

Juicy tomatoes and crisp okra are charred on the grill and tossed in fresh herbs for a salad that's made up of only the good stuff.

½	pound okra, halved lengthwise
½	cup sliced red onion
⅓	cup plus 1 tablespoon olive oil, divided
3	cloves garlic, thinly sliced
2	medium heirloom tomatoes, quartered
2	clusters grape tomatoes on the vine
⅓	cup chopped fresh herbs (such as parsley, basil, thyme, and oregano)
1	teaspoon lime zest
2	tablespoons fresh lime juice
1	tablespoon red wine vinegar
2	cloves garlic, grated
1½	teaspoons kosher salt
¼	teaspoon Slap Ya Mama Original Blend Cajun Seasoning

Garnish: chopped fresh herbs, freshly cracked black pepper

1. Heat a 12-inch cast-iron skillet over high heat on a grill. Working in batches, add okra in a single layer; cook, without stirring, until charred. Transfer to a serving platter, and set aside. Brush onion with 1 tablespoon oil, and add onion and sliced garlic to skillet; cook until lightly charred. Transfer to serving platter. Place heirloom tomatoes on grill, and cook until charred; place on serving platter. Add tomatoes on the vine, and cook until charred; set aside.

2. In a large bowl, whisk together herbs, lime zest and juice, vinegar, grated garlic, salt, Slap Ya Mama Original Blend Cajun Seasoning, and remaining ⅓ cup oil. Toss with okra, onion, and heirloom tomatoes. Serve with grilled tomatoes on the vine. Garnish with herbs and freshly cracked black pepper, if desired.

FRENCH ONION SOUP

MAKES 8 SERVINGS

Few things can't be solved over a steaming bowl of French onion soup. Let your troubles melt away with your first taste of this warm broth topped with baguette rounds and Swiss cheese.

- ½ cup unsalted butter
- 2 teaspoons sugar
- 8 large yellow onions, thinly sliced
- 1 tablespoon minced garlic
- 2 tablespoons all-purpose flour
- 6 cups beef broth
- 1 (10.5-ounce) can beef consommé
- 1½ teaspoons kosher salt
- 1 teaspoon ground black pepper
- ½ teaspoon Slap Ya Mama White Pepper Blend Seasoning
- 1 tablespoon chopped fresh thyme
- Toasted baguette rounds
- Shredded Swiss cheese
- Garnish: fresh thyme

1. In a large Dutch oven, melt butter over medium heat. Add sugar and onions, in batches if necessary; cook, stirring frequently, until onion is golden brown, about 1 hour.
2. Add garlic, and cook for 2 minutes. Stir in flour, and cook for 2 minutes. Stir in beef broth, beef consommé, salt, pepper, and Slap Ya Mama White Pepper Blend Seasoning; bring to a boil. Reduce heat to medium-low, and simmer for 30 minutes.
3. Preheat oven to broil.
4. Add thyme to soup, and simmer for 5 minutes. Ladle soup into ovenproof serving bowls; top with baguette rounds and cheese.
5. Broil 6 inches from heat until cheese is browned and bubbly, about 3 minutes. Garnish with thyme, if desired.

HOMEMADE VEGETABLE SOUP

MAKES 12 SERVINGS

Your favorite vegetables are cooked in tomato sauce and Slap Ya Mama Original Blend Cajun Seasoning for an extra kick. Try adding noodles for an even heartier meal.

8   cups water
1   pound beef stew meat or cubed ham
Slap Ya Mama Original Blend Cajun Seasoning, to taste
3   (8-ounce) cans tomato sauce
3   medium russet potatoes, peeled and cubed
2   cups carrot, chopped
1   large onion, chopped
1   large bell pepper, chopped
2   tablespoons minced garlic
1   (16-ounce) can corn kernels
1   (16-ounce) can green beans
1   (14.5-ounce) can beef broth
1   (10.75-ounce) can cream of mushroom soup
1   (8.5-ounce) can peas and carrots
2   ounces uncooked spaghetti noodles (optional)
Garnish: chopped fresh parsley
Saltine crackers, to serve

1. In a large stockpot, bring 8 cups water to a boil over high heat. Season meat with Slap Ya Mama Original Blend Cajun Seasoning, and add to water; boil for about 10 minutes.
2. Reduce heat to medium-low; add tomato sauce, potatoes, carrot, onion, bell pepper, and garlic. Add more Slap Ya Mama Original Blend Cajun Seasoning, to taste; cook for 15 minutes.
3. Add corn, green beans, broth, soup, and canned peas and carrots. Add enough water to reach 2 to 3 inches from top of pot; cook for about 1 hour.
4. If adding noodles, break spaghetti up into short pieces, and add to soup. Cook for about 10 minutes. Garnish with parsley, if desired. Serve with saltine crackers.

COOKING TIP FROM MAMA JEN

About 10 to 15 minutes before serving sauces and soups, add chopped fresh parsley while the pot is simmering.

SKIRT STEAK SALAD

MAKES 4 SERVINGS

Baby romaine lettuce topped with skirt steak and crispy ciabatta croutons—this is one salad you won't be able to turn down.

1½	pounds skirt steak
	Slap Ya Mama Hot Blend Cajun Seasoning, to taste
4	tablespoons extra-virgin olive oil, divided
2	ciabatta rolls, cut into cubes (about 5 cups)
2	cloves garlic, finely minced
½	teaspoon Slap Ya Mama Original Blend Cajun Seasoning, plus more to taste
6	cups fresh baby romaine lettuce
2	cups cherry tomatoes, halved
½	cup thinly sliced radishes
½	cup small fresh basil leaves
2	tablespoons capers
2	tablespoons brine from caper jar

1. Season steak with Slap Ya Mama Hot Blend Cajun Seasoning, to taste, and set aside.
2. In a large nonstick skillet, heat 1 tablespoon oil over medium-high heat. Add bread cubes; cook, turning as needed, until crisp and slightly golden, about 5 minutes. Add garlic and ½ teaspoon Slap Ya Mama Original Blend Cajun Seasoning; cook, tossing constantly, until garlic is slightly golden, about 30 seconds. Transfer to a large bowl; wipe skillet clean.
3. In same skillet, heat 1 tablespoon oil over medium-high heat. Add steak; sear until browned on bottom, about 4 minutes. Turn, and sear until browned on other side, 3 to 4 minutes. Transfer steak to a cutting board, and let rest for 5 minutes.
4. In a large bowl, combine romaine, tomatoes, radishes, basil, capers, caper brine, and remaining 2 tablespoons oil. Toss to coat romaine and vegetables, and season with a little Slap Ya Mama Original Blend Cajun Seasoning, to taste.
5. Divide salad and croutons among serving plates. Thinly slice steak against the grain, and divide among plates.

HEARTY BEEF & BEAN CHILI

MAKES 6 TO 8 SERVINGS

On a cold day, there is nothing better than a bowl of homemade chili spiced up with Slap Ya Mama seasonings. For the Walker family, this chili hits the spot whenever the temperatures drop.

- 1 pound beef sirloin steak, diced
- 1 teaspoon Slap Ya Mama Hot Blend Cajun Seasoning
- 1 tablespoon olive oil
- 1 pound ground round beef
- 1 yellow onion, chopped
- 1 green bell pepper, chopped
- 3 cloves garlic, minced
- 1 jalapeño, chopped
- 2 (8-ounce) cans tomato sauce
- 1 (15-ounce) can kidney beans, drained and rinsed
- 1 (15-ounce) can pinto beans, drained and rinsed
- 1 (10-ounce) can tomatoes with green chiles
- 1 (6-ounce) can tomato paste
- ½ cup beef broth
- ½ cup water
- 2 tablespoons Slap Ya Mama Cajun Pepper Sauce
- 2 teaspoons Slap Ya Mama Original Blend Cajun Seasoning
- 2 teaspoons chili powder
- 1 teaspoon ground cumin
- 1 teaspoon ground oregano
- Garnish: shredded Cheddar cheese, chopped green onion

1. Sprinkle beef sirloin steak with Slap Ya Mama Hot Blend Cajun Seasoning.

2. In a large Dutch oven, heat oil over medium-high heat. Add sirloin steak and ground round beef; cook, stirring frequently, until browned. Add onion, bell pepper, garlic, and jalapeño; cook until softened. Reduce heat to medium; stir in tomato sauce, beans, tomatoes with green chiles, tomato paste, broth, ½ cup water, Slap Ya Mama Cajun Pepper Sauce, Slap Ya Mama Original Blend Cajun Seasoning, chili powder, cumin, and oregano. Bring to a light boil; reduce heat, cover, and simmer, stirring occasionally, for 30 minutes.

3. Ladle chili into serving bowls. Garnish with cheese and green onion, if desired.

MAMA JEN'S POTATO SALAD

MAKES ABOUT 18 SERVINGS

Mama Jen is known for her potato salad served at family gatherings. We just can't get enough of it!

1 (5-pound) bag yellow potatoes
Kosher salt
10 hard-boiled eggs, peeled and chopped
1 cup mayonnaise, plus more if needed
½ cup sweet pickle relish
½ medium onion, chopped small
½ medium green bell pepper, chopped small
2 tablespoons yellow mustard
2 teaspoons Slap Ya Mama Signature Blend Garlic Salt
Slap Ya Mama Original Blend Cajun Seasoning, to taste

1. Rinse potatoes and cut off any dark spots and leave skin on. Cut into bite-size cubes. In a large pot, bring potatoes, salt, and water to cover to a boil over medium-high heat; cook until tender, about 25 minutes. Drain the potatoes once they are done.

2. In a large bowl, add potatoes and eggs, stirring to combine. Then, add all remaining ingredients. Mix up and taste. Add more mayonnaise and seasoning, if needed. Refrigerate in an airtight container.

SMOKY CHICKEN SALAD

MAKES ABOUT 4½ CUPS

Quick and easy, this chicken salad is always a big hit.

- 4 cups shredded smoked chicken
- 1 (15-ounce) can black-eyed peas, drained and rinsed
- 8 ounces grape tomatoes, halved
- ¼ cup mayonnaise
- ¼ cup sour cream
- 1 teaspoon Slap Ya Mama Original Blend Cajun Seasoning
- ¼ teaspoon liquid smoke
- Assorted crackers, to serve

1. In a large bowl, stir together chicken, peas, tomatoes, mayonnaise, sour cream, Slap Ya Mama Original Blend Cajun Seasoning, and liquid smoke until well combined. Refrigerate until ready to serve, at least 1 hour. Serve with crackers.

CREAMY SWEET POTATO SOUP

MAKES 4 TO 6 SERVINGS

Crispy tasso ham tops this creamy soup for the perfect weeknight meal.

4 tablespoons olive oil, divided
1 cup finely chopped tasso ham
1 medium yellow onion, chopped
1½ teaspoons kosher salt
¼ teaspoon ground black pepper
1½ pounds diced peeled sweet potatoes (about 2 large potatoes)
1 medium green apple, peeled and chopped
1 teaspoon smoked paprika
1 teaspoon chopped garlic
1 teaspoon chopped fresh ginger
4 cups vegetable broth
¼ cup heavy whipping cream
1 teaspoon Slap Ya Mama Original Blend Cajun Seasoning
Garnish: chopped fresh parsley
Crusty rolls, to serve

1. In a large Dutch oven, heat 3 tablespoons oil over medium heat. Add tasso, and cook, stirring occasionally, until golden brown and crispy, 5 to 7 minutes. Remove tasso using a slotted spoon, and let drain on paper towels. Strain drippings though a fine-mesh sieve, reserving drippings.
2. In same pot, heat remaining 1 tablespoon oil over medium heat. Add onion, salt, and pepper, and cook, stirring occasionally, until onion is softened and lightly golden brown, 7 to 10 minutes. Stir in sweet potatoes, apple, paprika, garlic, and ginger. Cook, stirring occasionally, until potatoes and apples begin to soften, 7 to 10 minutes. Stir in broth, and bring to a boil. Reduce heat, and simmer, stirring occasionally, until potatoes and apples are very tender, 15 to 20 minutes.
3. Stir cream and Slap Ya Mama Original Blend Cajun Seasoning into potato mixture. Using an immersion blender, blend until very smooth. (Alternatively, transfer soup, in batches if necessary, to the container of a blender. Secure lid on blender, and remove center piece of lid to let steam escape; place a clean towel over opening in lid to avoid splatters. Process until very smooth.)
4. Top with tasso and reserved drippings. Garnish with parsley. Serve with bread.

PICKLED OKRA SUCCOTASH SALAD

MAKES 4 TO 6 SERVINGS

Full of fresh produce, this salad is a hit at every family potluck.

4	ears fresh corn
1	medium red bell pepper, halved
2	cups cherry tomatoes, halved
1	cup cooked Fordhook lima beans, drained
¾	cup sliced pickled okra
½	cup ½-inch sliced green onion
½	cup extra-virgin olive oil
5	tablespoons pickled okra brine
1½	teaspoons honey
1	teaspoon packed chopped fresh dill
1	teaspoon minced garlic
1½	teaspoons Slap Ya Mama White Pepper Blend Seasoning
½	teaspoon lemon zest
½	teaspoon fresh lemon juice
¼	teaspoon paprika
5	slices thick-cut smoked bacon, fully cooked

Garnish: chopped fresh dill

1. Heat a cast-iron grill pan over medium-high heat. Lightly spray pan with cooking spray. Grill corn, turning frequently, until charred and tender, about 15 minutes. Let cool enough to handle; cut kernels off cob to measure 2 cups. Let cool completely.
2. Lightly spray grill pan with cooking spray again. Place bell pepper, cut side up, in pan, and grill until just charred and tender, about 5 minutes, turning once halfway through. Let cool completely, and chop bell pepper.
3. In a large bowl, combine corn, bell pepper, tomatoes, beans, okra, and green onion.
4. In a small bowl, whisk together oil, okra brine, honey, dill, garlic, Slap Ya Mama White Pepper Blend Seasoning, lemon zest and juice, and paprika. Pour over corn mixture, tossing to coat. Crumble cooked bacon over salad. Garnish with dill, if desired. Serve immediately.

GRILLED VEGETABLES AND ZESTY RICE SALAD

MAKES 6 TO 8 SERVINGS

Fresh veggies, herbs, and a tangy dressing combine for the perfect light lunch or side dish.

2	red bell peppers, halved
2	green bell peppers, halved
2	jalapeños, halved and seeded
2	bunches green onions
1	cup crumbled feta cheese
1	cup chopped toasted pecans
¼	cup chopped fresh parsley
1	tablespoon chopped fresh dill
1	tablespoon olive oil
½	teaspoon lemon zest
1	tablespoon fresh lemon juice
1	teaspoon Slap Ya Mama Original Blend Cajun Seasoning
1	teaspoon dried Italian seasoning
4	cups cooked long-grain white rice

1. Preheat grill to medium-high heat (350° to 400°).

2. Grill bell peppers, jalapeños, and green onion, turning occasionally, until browned and lightly charred, 5 to 10 minutes. Let cool completely. Chop into small pieces.

3. In a large bowl, combine grilled vegetables, feta, pecans, parsley, dill, oil, lemon zest and juice, Slap Ya Mama Original Blend Cajun Seasoning, and Italian seasoning. Add rice, and stir until combined. Cover and refrigerate until ready to serve, or up to 2 days.

CHAPTER FOUR

SANDWICHES & PO' BOYS

Authentic Louisiana sandwiches at their best

FRIED SHRIMP PO' BOYS

MAKES 4

This fried shrimp po' boy is full of Cajun flavor. The Slap Ya Mama Cajun Fish Fry and Slap Ya Mama Cajun Pepper Sauce spice things up for added deliciousness.

Vegetable oil, for frying
2 large eggs
¼ cup whole milk
1 (12-ounce) box Slap Ya Mama Cajun Fish Fry
1½ pounds medium fresh shrimp, peeled and deveined
6 tablespoons unsalted butter, melted
4 (8-inch) loaves French bread, halved lengthwise
Rémoulade Sauce (recipe follows)
Toppings: shredded iceberg lettuce, sliced dill pickles, sliced tomatoes, Slap Ya Mama Cajun Pepper Sauce

1. Preheat oven to 350°.
2. In a heavy stockpot or deep skillet, pour oil to a depth of 2 inches, and heat over medium heat until a deep-fry thermometer registers 350°.
3. In a small bowl, whisk together eggs and milk. In a medium bowl, place Slap Ya Mama Cajun Fish Fry. Dip shrimp in egg mixture, letting excess drip off. Dredge in fish fry, coating completely. Working in batches, fry shrimp, stirring occasionally, until golden brown, about 4 minutes. Let drain on paper towels.
4. Spread melted butter onto cut sides of bread. Place on a baking sheet, cut sides up.
5. Bake for about 10 minutes.
6. Generously spread Rémoulade Sauce onto cut sides of bread. Layer with lettuce, pickles, tomatoes, and shrimp. Douse with Slap Ya Mama Cajun Pepper Sauce. Cover with top half of French bread, Rémoulade sauce side down.

Note: If you like it a little spicier, try seasoning the shrimp with Slap Ya Mama Hot Blend Cajun Seasoning before dipping them into the egg mixture.

RÉMOULADE SAUCE
MAKES ABOUT 1½ CUPS

1½ cups mayonnaise
2 tablespoons finely chopped fresh parsley
1½ tablespoons capers, chopped
1½ tablespoons Dijon mustard
2 teaspoons white wine vinegar
½ teaspoon Slap Ya Mama Cajun Hot Sauce
½ teaspoon kosher salt
¼ teaspoon ground black pepper

1. In a medium bowl, combine all ingredients. Cover and refrigerate for up to 3 days.

FRIED CATFISH PO' BOYS

MAKES 4

Put your fish fry to good use by dredging the catfish, slathering it in Rémoulade Sauce, and creating this delicious sandwich.

Vegetable oil, for frying
1   (12-ounce) box Slap Ya Mama Cajun Fish Fry
2   large eggs
1   tablespoon water
4   catfish fillets
2   cups Rémoulade Sauce (recipe on page 111)
4   (6- to 8-inch) loaves French bread, halved lengthwise
1   cup shredded iceberg lettuce
1   large beefsteak tomato, sliced

1. In a large Dutch oven, pour oil to a depth of 4 inches, and heat over medium heat until a deep-fry thermometer registers 350°.
2. In a medium bowl, place Slap Ya Mama Cajun Fish Fry. In a small bowl, whisk together eggs and 1 tablespoon water. Dip fish in egg mixture, letting excess drip off. Dredge in fish fry, coating completely. Working in batches, fry fish until golden brown, 2 to 4 minutes. Let drain on paper towels.
3. Using a spatula, spread ¼ cup Rémoulade Sauce onto bottom half of each loaf. Top with fried fish, lettuce, and tomato. Pour an additional ¼ cup Rémoulade Sauce over each sandwich. Cover with top halves of loaves.

COOKING TIP FROM MAMA JEN

When cooking, always remain well balanced with your spoon in one hand and your favorite beverage in the other.

DEBRIS PO' BOYS

MAKES 4

All the spices and flavors of chuck roast are combined with sandwich fixin's and fresh rolls—lunch is served.

1	(2.5-pound) beef chuck roast	1	cup chicken stock
2	cloves garlic, thinly sliced	2	tablespoons Worcestershire sauce
1	teaspoon Slap Ya Mama Original Blend Cajun Seasoning	1	tablespoon Slap Ya Mama Cajun Hot Sauce
1	teaspoon kosher salt	2	sprigs fresh thyme
½	teaspoon ground black pepper	1	dried bay leaf
3	tablespoons vegetable oil	1	cup mayonnaise
1	cup diced onion	4	ciabatta rolls, halved
½	cup diced carrot	1	cup shredded iceberg lettuce
1	cup beef stock	1	large beefsteak tomato, sliced

1. Make small cuts about every 3 inches into roast, being careful not to pierce through to bottom; insert garlic slices into cuts. Sprinkle both sides of roast with Slap Ya Mama Original Blend Cajun Seasoning, salt, and pepper.

2. In a large Dutch oven, heat oil over high heat until almost smoking. Carefully add roast; cook until well-browned on all sides. Remove from pan; reduce heat to medium. Add onion and carrot; cook until onion is tender, about 5 minutes. Return roast to pan; add stocks, Worcestershire, Slap Ya Mama Cajun Hot Sauce, thyme, and bay leaf. Bring to a boil; reduce heat to low. Cover and simmer until meat is fork-tender, about 3 hours. Using 2 forks, shred beef.

3. Using a spatula, spread mayonnaise onto bottom half of each roll. Top with lettuce and tomato. Spoon roast beef with gravy on top. Cover with top half of roll.

COOKING TIP FROM MAMA JEN

After slicing your roast, turkey, or chicken, place it back in the gravy to keep it moist.

FRIED CHICKEN CLUB SANDWICHES

MAKES 8

While it's impossible to get tired of fried chicken, you can shake things up by covering it in C'est Bon Slaw to create a deep-fried club sandwich.

- 2 cups whole buttermilk
- 1 tablespoon Slap Ya Mama Cajun Hot Sauce
- 8 chicken cutlets (about 4 pounds)
- Canola oil, for frying
- 3 cups all-purpose flour
- 3 tablespoons Slap Ya Mama Original Blend Cajun Seasoning
- 8 teaspoons Creole mustard
- 8 hamburger buns, halved
- C'est Bon Slaw (recipe follows)

1. In a 13x9-inch baking dish, combine buttermilk and Slap Ya Mama Cajun Hot Sauce. Add chicken to dish, making sure meat is submerged. Cover with plastic wrap, and refrigerate for at least 4 hours.

2. In a large cast-iron skillet, pour oil to a depth of 1 inch, and heat over medium heat until a deep-fry thermometer registers 350°.

3. In another 13x9-inch baking dish, stir together flour and Slap Ya Mama Original Blend Cajun Seasoning. Remove chicken from buttermilk mixture, discarding marinade. Dredge chicken in flour mixture, turning to coat. Working in batches, fry chicken until browned on both sides and a meat thermometer inserted in thickest portion registers 160°. Let drain on paper towels.

4. Spread 1 teaspoon mustard onto bottom half of each bun. Top with a fried chicken cutlet and C'est Bon Slaw. Cover with top half of bun.

C'EST BON SLAW

MAKES ABOUT 4 CUPS

- 4 cups thinly sliced green cabbage
- 1 cup thinly sliced red cabbage
- ½ cup grated carrot
- ½ cup thinly sliced onion
- ½ cup mayonnaise
- 3 tablespoons apple cider vinegar
- 1½ teaspoons sugar
- 1 teaspoon Creole mustard
- ¾ teaspoon celery salt
- ¼ teaspoon ground black pepper
- ¼ teaspoon Slap Ya Mama White Pepper Blend Seasoning

1. In a large bowl, combine cabbages, carrot, and onion.

2. In a small bowl, whisk together mayonnaise and all remaining ingredients. Pour mayonnaise mixture over cabbage mixture, stirring to combine. Refrigerate until ready to serve.

COOKING TIP FROM MAMA JEN

Teach your children to cook, and they will feed you when you're old.

MUFFULETTAS

MAKES 8

Not your average deli meat sandwich—layers of meat, cheese, and olives are served up on fresh bread to create this instant favorite.

- 2 (9-inch) round loaves muffuletta bread*, halved crosswise
- ½ pound thinly sliced salami
- ½ pound thinly sliced capicola
- ½ pound thinly sliced mortadella
- ½ pound thinly sliced soppressata
- ½ pound thinly sliced provolone cheese
- 5 cups prepared olive salad
- ¼ teaspoon Slap Ya Mama Low Sodium Cajun Seasoning

Garnish: Slap Ya Mama Green Pepper Sauce

1. On bottom half of each bread loaf, layer salami, capicola, mortadella, soppressata, and cheese.
2. Stir together olive salad and Slap Ya Mama Low Sodium Cajun Seasoning. Spoon over cheese. Cover with top half of loaf. Garnish with a few dashes of Slap Ya Mama Green Pepper Sauce, if desired.
3. Slice sandwiches into quarters. (Muffulettas may be made up to 3 hours ahead; wrap securely, and refrigerate until ready to serve.)

*We used Leidenheimer muffuletta bread.

CAJUN BURGERS

MAKES 6

Next time you're craving a burger, make it a Cajun! Spice up your patties, and serve them hot off the grill.

- 1 pound lean ground beef
- 1 pound ground pork
- ½ small onion, chopped
- ½ small bell pepper, chopped
- 3 tablespoons Worcestershire sauce
- 3 tablespoons Slap Ya Mama Cajun Pepper Sauce
- Slap Ya Mama Original Blend Cajun Seasoning, to taste
- 6 slices American or Cheddar cheese
- 6 hamburger buns, halved
- Lettuce, tomato, and ketchup, to serve

1. Preheat grill to high heat (400° to 450°).
2. In a large bowl, stir together beef, pork, onion, bell pepper, Worcestershire, Slap Ya Mama Cajun Pepper Sauce, and Slap Ya Mama Original Blend Cajun Seasoning until well combined. Divide mixture into 6 portions, and shape each portion into a large patty.
3. Grill burger patties to desired degree of doneness. Melt cheese on burgers during last minute of cooking, if desired. Serve burgers on buns. Serve with lettuce, tomato, and ketchup, if desired.

COOKING TIP FROM MAMA JEN

Stretch your favorite Koozie over a clean, empty pickle or roux jar for a great insulated drinking glass.

SPICY BACON AND POBLANO GRILLED CHEESE

MAKES 4

Melty cheese, fresh poblano peppers, and crispy bacon make for the best grilled cheese you'll ever have.

- 4 medium poblano peppers
- 8 slices farmhouse sandwich bread
- 8 slices Monterey Jack cheese with peppers
- 12 slices thick-cut peppered bacon, cooked until crisp
- 8 slices Muenster cheese
- 4 tablespoons Cajun Butter (recipe follows), divided

1. Heat a 12-inch cast-iron skillet over medium-high heat. Add peppers; cook, turning occasionally, until charred on all sides, 8 to 10 minutes. Place peppers in a medium bowl; cover with plastic wrap. Let cool enough to handle. Peel peppers, discarding skin. Split peppers lengthwise, discarding stems and seeds.

2. Layer 4 bread slices each with 2 slices Jack cheese, 3 slices cooked bacon, 1 poblano, 2 slices Muenster, and 1 bread slice. Brush outside of bread with a thin layer of Cajun Butter.

3. In same skillet, melt 2 tablespoons Cajun Butter over medium heat. Add 2 sandwiches; cook until cheese is melted and bread is toasted, 3 to 4 minutes per side. Repeat with remaining 2 tablespoons Cajun Butter and remaining 2 sandwiches. Serve immediately.

CAJUN BUTTER

MAKES ½ CUP

- ½ cup unsalted butter, softened
- 4 teaspoons Slap Ya Mama Original Blend Cajun Seasoning

1. In a small bowl, stir together all ingredients until well combined.

STEAK SANDWICHES

MAKES 4

This is one of our favorite sandwiches to enjoy on a Friday night. One bite and you'll be hooked.

1½	pounds flank steak
1	tablespoon Slap Ya Mama Signature Blend Steakhouse Seasoning
2	large white onions, thinly sliced
2	tablespoons unsalted butter
3	teaspoons Slap Ya Mama Signature Blend Chili Lime Seasoning, divided
⅓	cup mayonnaise
4	(6-inch) deli hoagie rolls, split on top
1	(8-ounce) package extra-sharp white Cheddar cheese, thinly sliced

1. Preheat grill to high (400° to 450°).
2. Rub steak evenly with Slap Ya Mama Signature Blend Steakhouse Seasoning. Let stand for 30 minutes.
3. Grill steak with grill lid covered until desired degree of doneness, turning occasionally, about 6 to 8 minutes per side. Let stand for 15 minutes. Thinly slice steak against the grain.
4. In a large skillet, cook onion over medium heat until beginning to caramelize, 15 to 20 minutes. Stir in butter and 2 teaspoons Slap Ya Mama Signature Blend Chili Lime Seasoning until butter is melted. Remove from heat.
5. Preheat oven to 450°.
6. In a small bowl, whisk together mayonnaise and remaining 1 teaspoon Slap Ya Mama Signature Blend Chili Lime Seasoning. Spread mayonnaise mixture evenly inside and outside rolls. Evenly divide steak in rolls. Top evenly with onions and cheese.
7. Bake until cheese is melted, about 5 minutes. Serve warm.

BLACKENED GROUPER SANDWICHES
MAKES 4

Blackened foods are a family favorite and beloved by many in Louisiana. Our Slap Ya Mama Signature Blend Blackened Seasoning has just the right blend of spices to give each fillet that ideal, zesty bite.

- ½ cup mayonnaise
- 2 tablespoons plus ½ teaspoon Slap Ya Mama Signature Blend Blackened Seasoning, divided
- 2 tablespoons sliced green onion
- ½ teaspoon lime zest
- 1 tablespoon fresh lime juice
- 4 (4-ounce) grouper fillets
- 2 tablespoons unsalted butter, melted
- 1 tablespoon vegetable oil
- 4 lime wedges
- 4 ciabatta rolls, buttered and toasted

Lettuce leaves, tomato slices, red onion slices, and pickles, to serve

1. In a medium bowl, whisk together mayonnaise, ½ teaspoon Slap Ya Mama Signature Blend Blackened Seasoning, green onion, lime zest, and juice. Cover and refrigerate until ready to use.

2. Brush both sides of fish with melted butter. Sprinkle remaining 2 tablespoons Slap Ya Mama Signature Blend Blackened Seasoning over both sides of fish.

3. In a large cast-iron skillet, heat oil over medium-high heat; add fish. Cook until fish flakes easily with a fork, about 3 minutes per side. Squeeze lime wedges over fish. Remove from skillet.

4. Spread cut sides of rolls with mayonnaise mixture. Top bottom halves of rolls with fish. Serve with lettuce, tomato, onion, and pickles. Cover with roll tops.

CHAPTER FIVE
SEAFOOD ENTRÉES

The stars of the show

CRAWFISH ÉTOUFFÉE

MAKES 6 SERVINGS

Crawfish tails cooked in vegetables and spices, served over hot rice—what could be better to serve to the ones you love?

1	cup unsalted butter, divided
1	large yellow onion, diced
1	large green bell pepper, seeded and diced
3	stalks celery, diced
1	tomato, diced
1	tablespoon minced garlic
½	cup seafood stock
1	(16-ounce) package cooked crawfish tails
1½	teaspoons Slap Ya Mama Original Blend Cajun Seasoning
2	teaspoons Slap Ya Mama Cajun Hot Sauce

Hot cooked rice, to serve
Garnish: chopped fresh parsley, chopped green onion

1. In a large Dutch oven, heat ¼ cup butter over medium heat. Add onion, bell pepper, celery, and tomato; cook until tender. Add garlic; cook for 2 minutes. Add stock; bring to a boil over high heat. Reduce heat, and simmer until liquid is reduced by half, 15 to 20 minutes. Add crawfish, and stir to combine. Add Slap Ya Mama Original Blend Cajun Seasoning and Slap Ya Mama Cajun Hot Sauce. Taste, and adjust seasonings, if necessary.

2. Cut remaining ¾ cup butter into cubes. Remove pan from heat; fold in cubed butter, stirring until a creamy sauce forms. Serve over hot cooked rice. Garnish with parsley and green onion, if desired.

BBQ SHRIMP

MAKES 4 SERVINGS

Jumbo shrimp served in a buttery, fragrant sauce calls for plenty of French bread to go around. You won't want to leave a single drop behind.

- 2 pounds head-on jumbo or colossal fresh shrimp
- 7 cups cold water
- 12 tablespoons unsalted butter, divided
- 2 shallots, minced
- 4 cloves garlic, minced
- 2 tablespoons finely chopped fresh rosemary
- 2 teaspoons Slap Ya Mama Original Blend Cajun Seasoning
- 1½ teaspoons ground black pepper
- ¼ cup Worcestershire sauce
- ¼ cup Slap Ya Mama Cajun Hot Sauce
- 2 tablespoons fresh lemon juice
- ½ cup dark or amber beer
- 2 loaves French bread, to serve

1. Peel and devein shrimp, leaving tails on and reserving heads and shells. Refrigerate shrimp.
2. In a small Dutch oven, bring shrimp heads and shells and 7 cups cold water to a boil over medium-high heat. Reduce heat to medium, and cook, stirring occasionally, for 15 minutes. Skim any froth as it rises to surface. Strain through a fine-mesh sieve into a bowl, and set aside. Reserve 1 cup shrimp stock. Remaining stock can be refrigerated for up to 1 week or frozen for up to 3 months.
3. In a large skillet, melt 5 tablespoons butter over high heat. Add shallot, garlic, rosemary, Slap Ya Mama Original Blend Cajun Seasoning, and pepper; cook, stirring constantly, until fragrant, about 1 minute. Add reserved 1 cup stock, Worcestershire, Slap Ya Mama Cajun Hot Sauce, and lemon juice, stirring to combine. Add shrimp; cook just until pink and firm. Add beer, and cook for 2 to 3 minutes. Reduce heat to low, and add remaining 7 tablespoons butter. Gently stir as butter melts into sauce and sauce is emulsified. Serve immediately with French bread.

SHRIMP & GRITS

MAKES 4 SERVINGS

Whether it's Sunday brunch or Wednesday night supper, shrimp and grits is always a good call. Cheesy grits covered in bacon, tasso, and jumbo shrimp—you gotta love that.

- 4 cups water
- 1 cup stone-ground grits
- 2 cups shredded Cheddar cheese
- 4 tablespoons unsalted butter, divided
- 2 teaspoons Slap Ya Mama Original Blend Cajun Seasoning
- ½ teaspoon kosher salt
- 1 pound jumbo fresh shrimp, peeled and deveined (tails left on)
- 1 teaspoon Slap Ya Mama White Pepper Blend Seasoning
- 6 slices thick-cut bacon, chopped
- ½ onion, chopped (about 1 cup)
- ½ green bell pepper, chopped (about ½ cup)
- ½ cup tasso or smoked ham, chopped
- 2 tablespoons chopped fresh parsley
- 2 tablespoons fresh lemon juice
- ½ teaspoon minced garlic

Garnish: chopped green onion

1. In a large stockpot, bring 4 cups water and grits to a boil over high heat. Reduce heat to low, and simmer, stirring frequently, until grits have absorbed water, 25 to 30 minutes. Remove from heat; add cheese, 3 tablespoons butter, Slap Ya Mama Original Blend Cajun Seasoning, and salt, stirring until cheese is melted.
2. Sprinkle shrimp with Slap Ya Mama White Pepper Blend Seasoning, and set aside.
3. In a large saucepan, cook bacon over medium-high heat until crisp, about 10 minutes. Remove bacon using a slotted spoon, and let drain on paper towels, reserving drippings in pan. Reduce heat to medium.
4. Add onion, bell pepper, and tasso to pan; cook until onion is translucent, about 7 minutes. Add shrimp; cook until pink and firm, about 4 minutes. Add bacon, parsley, lemon juice, garlic, and remaining 1 tablespoon butter; cook for about 3 minutes. Spoon grits into serving bowls, and generously top with shrimp mixture. Garnish with green onion, if desired.

BLACKENED REDFISH

MAKES 4 TO 6 SERVINGS

Spicy and fresh, there's nothing like the flavor that comes from cooking fish in a cast-iron skillet.

- ½ cup unsalted butter, melted
- 2 pounds redfish fillets
- 3 to 4 tablespoons Slap Ya Mama Signature Blend Blackened Seasoning
- 1 tablespoon olive oil
- 4 lemons, halved

1. Preheat grill to high heat (400° to 450°). Preheat a 12-inch cast-iron skillet on grill for 15 minutes.
2. Pour melted butter in a shallow dish. Dip each fillet in butter, turning to coat. Sprinkle both sides of fillets with Slap Ya Mama Signature Blend Blackened Seasoning; pat gently to coat.
3. Add oil to skillet (oil should smoke); place fish in skillet. Cook, covered, until browned, 3 to 4 minutes. Turn, and cook, covered, until fish flakes easily with a fork, 3 to 4 minutes. Carefully remove skillet from grill.
4. Place lemon halves, cut side down, on grill. Cook, covered, until charred, 3 to 4 minutes. Serve with fish.

FRIED CATFISH WITH CRAWFISH AU GRATIN

MAKES 4 SERVINGS

This creamy crawfish sauce combines with flaky fried catfish for a warm, satisfying meal that will have your family coming back for seconds.

CRAWFISH AU GRATIN SAUCE
- 7 tablespoons unsalted butter
- ¾ cup diced onion
- ¼ cup diced green bell pepper
- ¼ tablespoon minced garlic
- 5 tablespoons all-purpose flour
- 1 tablespoon Slap Ya Mama Original Blend Cajun Seasoning
- 1 tablespoon sugar
- ⅛ teaspoon dried basil
- Pinch dried thyme
- 3 cups whole milk
- ¼ cup white wine
- 4 ounces American cheese, cubed
- 1 pound cooked and peeled crawfish tails

FRIED CATFISH
- 4 (4-ounce) catfish fillets
- Slap Ya Mama Original Blend Cajun Seasoning, to taste
- 2 large eggs
- 1 cup whole milk
- 1½ cups Slap Ya Mama Cajun Fish Fry
- Canola oil, for frying

Garnish: sliced green onion

1. For crawfish: In a 12-inch skillet, melt butter over medium heat. Add onion, bell pepper, and garlic; cook until softened. Add flour, and stir until a blond roux forms, 2 to 3 minutes. Stir in Slap Ya Mama Original Blend Cajun Seasoning, sugar, basil, and thyme. Add milk and wine; cook, stirring constantly, until liquid thickens. Add cheese, and stir until cheese is melted and fully incorporated into sauce. Add crawfish tails; cook until heated through, about 4 minutes.

2. For catfish: Sprinkle catfish with Slap Ya Mama Original Blend Cajun Seasoning.

3. In a small bowl, whisk together eggs and milk. Place Slap Ya Mama Cajun Fish Fry in a medium bowl. Dip catfish in egg mixture, letting excess drip off. Dredge in fish fry, coating completely.

4. In a large skillet, pour oil to a depth of 4 inches, and heat over medium heat until a deep-fry thermometer registers 350°. Carefully place catfish in oil. Fry until golden brown, 6 to 8 minutes.

5. Place catfish on serving plates. Spoon crawfish au gratin over catfish. Garnish with green onion, if desired.

COOKING TIP FROM MAMA JEN

When eating crawfish, don't eat the ones with a straight tail. That means they were probably dead before they were boiled, and they don't taste as good.

CATFISH COURTBOUILLON

MAKES 8 TO 10 SERVINGS

Thick cross-section cuts of whole dressed catfish are covered in a quickly cooked broth that poaches the fish and creates a delicious dish.

- ¼ cup vegetable oil
- 6 catfish steaks (about 2 pounds)
- 1½ teaspoons Slap Ya Mama Original Blend Cajun Seasoning
- 1 large sweet onion, chopped
- 1 large green bell pepper, chopped
- 2 teaspoons minced garlic
- 2 (8-ounce) cans tomato sauce
- ½ cup chopped green onion
- ½ cup chopped fresh parsley
- Hot cooked rice, to serve

1. In a large cast-iron stockpot or Dutch oven, heat oil over low heat.
2. Sprinkle catfish with Slap Ya Mama Original Blend Cajun Seasoning; place fish in pot. Layer with onion, bell pepper, and garlic; top with tomato sauce. (Do not stir.) Cover and shake pot in a circular motion. Fish will put out a little water. If not enough, you can add a little. Cook, shaking pot occasionally, for 1 hour.
3. Add green onion and parsley; cook for 10 minutes. Serve over hot cooked rice.

COOKING TIP FROM MAMA JEN

When making any kind of tomato-based sauce, add a Hershey's kiss to neutralize the acid and decrease your chances of getting heartburn.

Y'ALL SUCK ON DEM HEADS!
THE CAJUN CRAWFISH SEASON

Native Americans were catching and eating crawfish for years before the Acadians arrived, although some legends tell of the northeastern lobster following the Acadians to Louisiana and shrinking in size over the long journey. The Acadians took quite well to the local crawfish, and they became a major part of the Cajun culture.

Crawfish—or mudbugs, as they are called since the popular species in Louisiana burrow into the wet ground of the freshwater bayous—can be boiled whole with spices and vegetables, or the tender meat can be featured in a variety of Cajun cuisine from étouffée to meat pies. Every spring when crawfish are in season, Louisiana families like the Walkers spend their afternoons gathered around picnic tables, picking crawfish. They spread old newspaper across long tables where they dump a giant pot of steaming crawfish along with boiled potatoes, garlic cloves, corn on the cob, whole mushrooms, and onions.

Some of the Walkers' fondest memories involve farming crawfish themselves. One of TW's clients had a crawfish pond. When TW's brother Bob was coming to Ville Platte for Easter with his family, TW asked his client if the kids could come by and pick up some crawfish with hand nets. "*Mais, cher,* don't worry about that," TW's client said, using the Cajun term of endearment. "I'll tell my guy not to make his run on Saturday morning, and y'all can just pick up all the traps."

TW couldn't believe this generous offer. He loaded up the whole family, and they headed to the ponds. "Jack and Joe were just waist-high then," recalls TW. "We pulled them behind us in a boat and waded through the water with our hip boots on, even Mama Jen. I think we came up with over 250 pounds of crawfish." A good rule of thumb is three pounds of crawfish per person, which means the Walkers hit the mother lode. "We got to be crawfish farmers for the day," Jack remembers fondly.

TW's client invited them back year after year. As Jack and Joe got older, they wore the snake-proof boots and started pulling the boats through the muddy water for the younger kids to ride. "It was always a good weekend," says TW. "It brought all the family together."

The Walkers took all those crawfish back to the

Bayou Chicot house and cooked them in the backyard under twinkle lights TW strung from the trees. "We ate for two hours, Cajun French music blaring in the background," says Bob. "Living in Mississippi, I wanted my kids to experience the way I grew up."

Today, when the Walkers eat crawfish, they all remember those Easter weekends. They pop off the head and suck the juices, peel off the shell and pop the meat in their mouths. The Slap Ya Mama seasoning tingles their lips just perfectly, and they're taken right back to those Easter weekends way back when.

CRAWFISH BOIL

MAKES ABOUT 12 SERVINGS

The quintessential Cajun meal—find a reason to celebrate and enjoy.

30 to 40 pounds live crawfish
6   cups kosher salt, divided
4   (1-pound) bags Slap Ya Mama Cajun Seafood Boil, divided
10 lemons, halved
10 pounds red potatoes, quartered
8   pounds corn, shucked and halved
16 heads garlic, halved crosswise
8   pounds andouille sausage, cut into thirds
Slap Ya Mama Original Blend Cajun Seasoning, to taste
Mama Jen's Cajun Crawfish Dipping Sauce (recipe follows)
Mama Jen's Spicy Cajun Seafood Dipping Sauce (recipe follows)

1. In a large bucket or cooler, place live crawfish, 3 cups salt, and water to cover. Let stand for 30 minutes, discarding any crawfish that float to the top (which indicates crawfish are dead). Rinse crawfish thoroughly using cold water.

2. In a large outdoor 60-gallon pot with a crawfish basket, place 2 bags Slap Ya Mama Cajun Seafood Boil, lemons (squeezing juices), and remaining 3 cups salt. Fill halfway with water, and bring to a boil over high heat on a heavy-duty outdoor burner. Add potatoes, corn, and garlic; return to a boil. Reduce heat, and simmer for 15 minutes.

3. Submerge crawfish, and add sausage and remaining 2 bags Slap Ya Mama Cajun Seafood Boil. Return water to a boil. Turn off heat, and cover. Let stand until crawfish are tender and float to top, about 30 minutes. Sprinkle with Slap Ya Mama Original Blend Cajun Seasoning to taste. Serve immediately with Mama Jen's Cajun Crawfish Dipping Sauce and Mama Jen's Spicy Cajun Seafood Dipping Sauce.

MAMA JEN'S CAJUN CRAWFISH DIPPING SAUCE
MAKES ABOUT 1 CUP

½   cup mayonnaise
¼   cup ketchup
1   tablespoon yellow mustard
1   tablespoon Slap Ya Mama Cajun Hot Sauce
1   teaspoon prepared horseradish
1   teaspoon minced garlic
2   teaspoons Worcestershire sauce
1   teaspoon Slap Ya Mama Original Blend Cajun Seasoning
1   tablespoon fresh lemon juice
½   teaspoon sugar

1. In a medium bowl, combine mayonnaise and ketchup. Add remaining ingredients, one at a time, and stir well. Refrigerate for at least 1 hour before using.

MAMA JEN'S SPICY CAJUN SEAFOOD DIPPING SAUCE

MAKES ABOUT ¾ CUP

- ½ cup ketchup
- 1 tablespoon Slap Ya Mama Cajun Hot Sauce
- 1 tablespoon Worcestershire sauce
- 1 teaspoon prepared horseradish
- 1 teaspoon Slap Ya Mama Original Blend Cajun Seasoning
- 1 teaspoon fresh lemon juice

1. In a small bowl, combine ketchup, Slap Ya Mama Cajun Hot Sauce, and Worcestershire. Add horseradish, Slap Ya Mama Original Blend Cajun Seasoning, and lemon juice, and stir well. Refrigerate for 1 hour before using.

SHRIMP FETTUCCINE

MAKES 6 SERVINGS

Noodles smothered in a creamy, cheesy sauce, this crowd-pleasing meal is the perfect way to feature fresh shrimp.

- ½ cup plus 2 tablespoons unsalted butter, divided
- 2 large onions, chopped
- 3 stalks celery, chopped
- 1 red bell pepper, seeded and chopped
- 4 cloves garlic, minced
- ½ cup chopped fresh parsley
- 1 cup sliced green onion, divided
- ¼ cup all-purpose flour
- 2 cups half-and-half
- ½ pound American cheese, cubed
- ½ pound Monterey Jack cheese with peppers, shredded
- 2 teaspoons Slap Ya Mama Original Blend Cajun Seasoning
- 2 pounds peeled and deveined fresh shrimp
- 1 (16-ounce) package fettuccine, cooked according to package directions
- 1 cup shredded Parmesan cheese

Garnish: chopped fresh parsley

1. In a large stockpot or Dutch oven, melt ½ cup butter over medium heat. Add onion; cook until translucent, about 7 minutes. Stir in celery, bell pepper, garlic, parsley, and ¾ cup green onion; cook until vegetables are softened, about 10 minutes.

2. Sprinkle flour over top vegetables, and stir for 1 minute. Reduce heat to medium-low, and slowly stir in half-and-half. Bring to a boil; reduce heat to low. Simmer until slightly thickened, about 4 minutes.

3. Slowly stir in American cheese, about ¼ cup at a time, letting each addition melt before adding the next; stir in Monterey Jack cheese in the same manner until incorporated. Stir in Slap Ya Mama Original Blend Cajun Seasoning.

4. In a large skillet, melt remaining 2 tablespoons butter over medium-high heat. Add shrimp, and cook until pink and firm, about 1 to 2 minutes per side.

5. Combine shrimp, cooked fettuccine, and sauce. Top with Parmesan and remaining ¼ cup green onion. Garnish with parsley, if desired. Serve immediately.

BOILED SHRIMP AND BOILED CRABS

When crawfish aren't in season, turn to shrimp and crabs for your backyard boils.

BOILED SHRIMP
MAKES 12 SERVINGS

- 1¼ cups plus 3 tablespoons Slap Ya Mama Cajun Seafood Boil, divided
- 1 lemon, halved
- 6 pounds jumbo fresh shrimp, unpeeled and head on
- Lemon wedges
- Cocktail sauce or butter sauce, to serve

1. Fill a large stockpot halfway full with water. Add 1¼ cups Slap Ya Mama Cajun Seafood Boil and lemon halves; bring to a rolling boil over high heat. Add shrimp; cover and return to a rolling boil. Uncover and boil for 3 to 4 minutes. Remove shrimp from pot; place in a large bowl or on a serving tray. Squeeze lemon wedges over shrimp, and sprinkle with remaining 3 tablespoons Slap Ya Mama Cajun Seafood Boil. Serve with cocktail sauce or butter sauce.

Note: You may also boil vegetables, such as corn, potatoes, sweet onions, whole garlic, and mushrooms. Boil veggies first, place in a large bowl, and cover with foil. Then, boil shrimp in the same water, adding a few more tablespoons Slap Ya Mama Cajun Seafood Boil to water before adding shrimp.

BOILED CRABS
MAKES 6 SERVINGS

- 4 quarts water
- 1 (1-pound) bag Slap Ya Mama Cajun Seafood Boil
- 2 tablespoons distilled white vinegar
- 2 lemons, halved
- 1 head garlic, cloves separated and peeled
- 4 bay leaves
- 4 dried chile peppers
- 3 sprigs fresh thyme
- ¼ cup sea salt
- 12 fresh crabs
- 3 pounds new potatoes, scrubbed clean
- 4 ears corn, shucked and cut into thirds
- 1 (10-ounce) bag pearl onions, peeled
- 1 (10-pound) bag ice

1. In a very large stockpot, bring 4 quarts water, Slap Ya Mama Cajun Seafood Boil, vinegar, lemons, garlic, bay leaves, chiles, thyme, and salt to a rolling boil over high heat. Add crabs, potatoes, corn, and onions; return to a rolling boil, and cook for 5 minutes. Turn off heat, and cover pot for 15 to 20 minutes.

2. Pour ice into pot. (This helps the crabs absorb the seasonings and prevents them from overcooking.) Let crabs stand in water for at least 1 hour before serving. Crabs can be served warm or completely cooled.

Note: Use about 3 tablespoons Slap Ya Mama Cajun Seafood Boil for every 1 pound of shrimp, crawfish, crab, or vegetable.

CRISPY CAJUN-FRIED ALLIGATOR

MAKES 4 TO 6 SERVINGS

Alligator is a staple in Louisiana households. When fried correctly, it'll taste just like chicken!

Vegetable oil, for frying
1   cup whole buttermilk
1   large egg
1   tablespoon Slap Ya Mama Jalapeño Pepper Sauce
1   pound alligator meat, cut into 1-inch cubes
2   cups all-purpose flour
1   tablespoon plus 2 teaspoons Slap Ya Mama White Pepper Blend Seasoning, divided
French fries and lemon wedges, to serve

1. In a medium Dutch oven, pour oil to a depth of 2 inches. Heat oil over medium heat until a deep-fry thermometer registers 350°.
2. In a medium bowl, whisk together buttermilk, egg, and Slap Ya Mama Jalapeño Pepper Sauce. Add alligator to buttermilk mixture.
3. In another bowl, whisk together flour and 1 tablespoon Slap Ya Mama White Pepper Blend Seasoning.
4. Working in batches, remove alligator from buttermilk mixture, letting excess drip off. Dredge in flour mixture, shaking off excess. Carefully drop into hot oil, and fry, turning occasionally, until golden brown and crispy, 2 to 3 minutes. Use a slotted spoon to remove alligator, and let drain on paper towels. Sprinkle with remaining 2 teaspoons Slap Ya Mama White Pepper Blend Seasoning. Serve with french fries and lemon.

CRUNCHY CATFISH TACOS WITH APPLE SLAW

MAKES 8

A crisp apple slaw and creamy chipotle mayonnaise add the perfect contrast to flaky, fried catfish.

- 1 cup mayonnaise
- 2 tablespoons honey
- 1 tablespoon fresh lime juice
- 1 tablespoon minced chipotle peppers in adobo sauce
- 2¼ teaspoons Slap Ya Mama Signature Blend Taco & Fajita Seasoning, divided
- Vegetable oil, for frying
- 1 cup all-purpose flour
- 1½ teaspoons kosher salt
- 1 teaspoon baking powder
- 1 cup club soda
- 1½ tablespoons Slap Ya Mama Cajun Hot Sauce
- 3 cups panko (Japanese bread crumbs)
- 4 (6-ounce) catfish fillets, cut into 2-inch pieces
- 8 (6-inch) flour tortillas
- Apple Slaw (recipe follows)
- Lime slices, to serve

1. In a medium bowl, stir together mayonnaise, honey, lime juice, chipotle in adobo, and ¼ teaspoon Slap Ya Mama Signature Blend Taco & Fajita Seasoning. Cover and refrigerate until ready to use.

2. Preheat oven to 200°.

3. In a large Dutch oven, pour oil to a depth of 4 inches, and heat over medium-high heat until a deep-fry thermometer registers 375°.

4. In a shallow dish, combine flour, salt, baking powder, and 1 teaspoon Slap Ya Mama Signature Blend Taco & Fajita Seasoning. Whisk in club soda and Slap Ya Mama Cajun Hot Sauce until smooth. In a separate shallow dish, whisk together bread crumbs and remaining 1 teaspoon Slap Ya Mama Signature Blend Taco & Fajita Seasoning.

5. Dip catfish pieces in batter, allowing excess to drip off; coat in bread crumbs.

6. Fry fish, in batches, until brown and crispy, 1 to 2 minutes per side. Transfer fish to a paper towel-lined baking sheet to drain, and keep warm in oven.

7. Spray both sides of tortillas with nonstick cooking spray. In a large skillet, cook tortillas over medium heat until lightly browned, 1 to 2 minutes per side.

8. To assemble, spread mayonnaise mixture onto one side of each tortilla, and top with Apple Slaw, fish pieces, and more mayonnaise mixture. Serve with lime.

APPLE SLAW

MAKES 8 SERVINGS

- 1 (10-ounce) bag angel hair coleslaw mix
- 1 Granny Smith apple, chopped
- 1 cup thinly sliced carrot
- ½ cup thinly sliced red onion
- 1 jalapeño, seeded and thinly sliced
- ¼ cup fresh lemon juice
- ¼ cup olive oil
- 2 teaspoons granulated sugar
- 1 teaspoon kosher salt
- ½ teaspoon Slap Ya Mama Signature Blend Taco & Fajita Seasoning

1. In a large bowl, combine slaw mix, apple, carrot, onion, and jalapeño.

2. In a small bowl, whisk together lemon juice, olive oil, sugar, salt, and Slap Ya Mama Signature Blend Taco & Fajita Seasoning. Pour dressing over slaw mixture, tossing to combine. Cover and refrigerate for at least 2 hours.

CHAPTER SIX
MEAT ENTRÉES
The main event

LIVING HIGH—AND LOW—ON THE HOG
SMOKED
SPECIALTY MEATS
THE CAJUN WAY

Cajuns love to pig out on pork, and the Walker family is no exception. From traditional gumbo with sausage to shrimp and corn soup with tasso ham, smoked pork provides protein and packs flavor into a variety of Cajun dishes.

"Living high on the hog," meaning to eat the highest-quality loin of the pig (located right above the belly), is a sign of prosperity. But ask even the wealthiest Cajuns, and they'll tell you they prefer boudin, ponce, and cracklin's, made from the scraps of the hog.

When the Acadians arrived in Louisiana, they had almost nothing. They had to use 100 percent of the valuable resources they could find. When they slaughtered a hog, they meticulously gleaned every part they could. They ground the scraps and mixed it with herbs, spices, and rice to create an assortment of sausage fillings and satisfying pork dishes. These resourceful Acadians took pork intestine, liver, and heart meat to create boudin. They stuffed sausage into the stomach lining of a pig to make ponce. They fried pork belly with the skin, and voilà, crispy cracklin's were born. Necessity is the mother of invention after all.

Walk into one of Louisiana's grocery stores, gas stations, or smoked meat shops, and you'll find an impressive display of unique Cajun meat products like hog's head cheese, stuffed beef tongue, marinated rabbit, golden fried boudin balls, and yards of smoked sausages. While these mom-and-pop meat markets are mind-boggling attractions for tourists, they are essential to the families of rural Louisiana towns.

"People in Ville Platte have to cook because there aren't a lot of restaurants here," says Jack. "You can't go have a nice Italian meal down the street or order a good steak, so you go to the meat market and make your own meals every night." Teet's Food Store, which bills itself as a "Spécialiste dans la Viande Boucanée," or a shop specializing in smoked meats, has been around since 1955. The family-owned business provides the Walkers with their smoked meats, and the store even created a signature sausage using Slap Ya Mama seasoning products.

"The original owner, Lawrence 'Teet' Deville, has passed away, but now, we work with his grandson, Luke, who runs the store with his father, Chris Deville," says Jack. "We use their ponce and tasso for Mama's recipes, or we might just throw some of their good sausage into a crawfish boil or grill it and serve it with mustard for an easy appetizer before dinner."

Even if you live far from Louisiana, you can place an online order with Teet's and have some of their Cajun specialty meats shipped right to your door.

PONCE SAUCE PIQUANTE

MAKES 8 SERVINGS

Essential to Cajun cuisine and its history, this classic Acadian dish uses smoked pork stomach sausage and other flavorful ingredients to create a rich, comforting meal.

- 1 pound smoked pork sausage, sliced
- 1 (10-ounce) can tomatoes with green chiles
- 2 teaspoons Slap Ya Mama Original Blend Cajun Seasoning
- 1 medium onion, chopped (about 1½ cups)
- 1 medium green bell pepper, chopped (about 1 cup)
- 2 teaspoons minced garlic (about 2 cloves)
- 1 (4-pound) smoked ponce
- 1 cup chopped green onion
- 1 cup chopped fresh parsley
- Hot cooked rice, to serve

1. In a large cast-iron stockpot or Dutch oven, heat sausage and water just to cover over medium-high heat. Cook, stirring frequently, until water is evaporated and sausage begins to brown, 2 to 3 minutes. Add more water until sausage is covered, and cook, stirring frequently, until no water is left.

2. Add tomatoes with chiles; cook with sausage and keep stirring until sausage is browned, about 10 minutes. Stir in Slap Ya Mama Original Blend Cajun Seasoning. Add onion, bell pepper, and garlic; cook, stirring frequently, for about 7 minutes. Stir in a little water. Add ponce, and add water until half of ponce is covered. Cover and cook over medium heat until tender, about 1 hour and 30 minutes, turning 3 or 4 times, and poking ponce with a skewer in several places to release juices.

3. Add green onion and parsley. Slice ponce in pot with gravy. Cover and simmer for 15 minutes. Serve over hot cooked rice.

CHICKEN SAUCE PIQUANTE

MAKES 4 TO 6 SERVINGS

Chicken Sauce Piquante is a traditional Cajun recipe that has been around for generations. With a reddish, spicy gravy, it has an incredible flavor and is fairly simple to prepare. Served over rice, this dish was and still is a staple in many households in and around the Acadiana area.

- 1 whole chicken, cut up (skin removed, if desired)
- 1 tablespoon plus 2 teaspoons Slap Ya Mama Original Blend Cajun Seasoning, divided
- 1 tablespoon Slap Ya Mama Cajun Pepper Sauce
- 2 tablespoons olive oil
- 1 sweet onion, chopped (about 1½ cups)
- 1 green bell pepper, chopped (about 1 cup)
- 4 cloves garlic, minced
- 1 (8-ounce) can tomato sauce
- ⅓ cup beef broth
- ⅓ cup heavy whipping cream
- ¼ cup diced mushrooms
- ¼ cup chopped green onion
- ¼ cup chopped fresh parsley
- Hot cooked rice, to serve

1. Season chicken with 2 teaspoons Slap Ya Mama Original Blend Cajun Seasoning and Slap Ya Mama Cajun Pepper Sauce.

2. In a 4-quart stockpot, heat oil over medium-high heat. Add chicken; cook until browned on all sides. (Don't be afraid to burn the chicken a little or for it to stick to the bottom of the pot. This is where the gravy will come from.) Remove chicken from pot.

3. Add onion, bell pepper, garlic, and just enough water to cover bottom of pot (about 1 cup); cook until vegetables are softened. Add tomato sauce; cook for 10 minutes. Add broth, cream, mushrooms, and remaining 1 tablespoon Slap Ya Mama Original Blend Cajun Seasoning; cook for 5 minutes. Reduce heat to medium; return chicken to pot, and fill pot with water just to top of chicken (about 1 quart). Cover and boil, stirring occasionally, until chicken is tender, about 1 hour.

4. Reduce heat, and uncover; stir in green onion and parsley. Simmer for 10 minutes. Serve over hot cooked rice.

Note: You may add smoked sausage to this dish. If you do, treat it just as you would

BEEF POT ROAST

MAKES 8 TO 10 SERVINGS

Nothing screams "feel-good food" more than a pot roast. Follow this easy recipe for a delicious beef pot roast the whole family will enjoy.

1	(3- to 4-pound) boneless beef chuck roast
12	cloves garlic, halved and divided
3	tablespoons Slap Ya Mama Original Blend Cajun Seasoning, divided
3	tablespoons olive oil, divided
1	large onion, quartered
1	large green bell pepper, seeded and chopped (about 1 cup)
10	medium whole carrots, peeled
½	cup water
8	small red potatoes
2	sprigs fresh thyme

1. Preheat oven to 350°.
2. Make 12 small cuts in roast just deep enough to insert half a clove of garlic (being careful not to pierce through to bottom). Insert half of garlic into cuts. Sprinkle both sides of roast with 2 tablespoons Slap Ya Mama Original Blend Cajun Seasoning.
3. In a large Dutch oven, heat 2 tablespoons oil over medium-high heat until almost smoking. Carefully add roast; cook until browned, 3 to 4 minutes per side. Remove roast, and set aside. (Some garlic will fall out; insert back into roast.)
4. Add remaining 1 tablespoon oil to pot. Add onion, bell pepper, carrots, and remaining garlic; cook until onion becomes slightly translucent and browned, about 8 minutes. Remove carrots, and set aside. Add ½ cup water; cook, scraping browned bits from bottom of Dutch oven with a wooden spoon. Add roast, carrots, potatoes, thyme, remaining 1 tablespoon Slap Ya Mama Original Blend Cajun Seasoning, and enough water to reach halfway up sides of roast. Bring to a boil; cover and place in oven.
5. Reduce oven temperature to 325°. Bake for 2 hours for a 3-pound roast or 3 hours for a 4-pound roast. Let stand for 10 minutes before serving.

COOKING TIP FROM MAMA JEN

The best pot scrubber is a heavy-duty, coarse stripping pad from the hardware store, usually found next to the sandpaper.

JAMBALAYA AND MAW MAW'S RED BEANS & RICE

Two great ways to prepare sausage and rice, these classic Cajun favorites are always sure to please.

JAMBALAYA

MAKES 6 TO 8 SERVINGS

- 1½ tablespoons vegetable oil
- 1 cup chopped sweet onion (about ½ large onion)
- ½ cup chopped green bell pepper (about ½ pepper)
- ¼ cup chopped celery (about 1 stalk)
- 1 tablespoon minced garlic (about 3 cloves)
- 8 ounces chopped smoked sausage
- 8 ounces chopped smoked tasso
- 1 (8-ounce) can tomatoes with green chiles
- 1 tablespoon Slap Ya Mama Cajun Pepper Sauce
- 2 teaspoons Slap Ya Mama Original Blend Cajun Seasoning
- 1 teaspoon kosher salt
- 1 teaspoon paprika
- 1 whole chicken, cooked and deboned
- 3½ cups chicken broth
- 2 cups medium-grain rice
- ½ cup minced fresh parsley
- ½ cup chopped green onion

1. In a large saucepan, heat oil over medium heat. Add onion, bell pepper, celery, and garlic; cook for 5 minutes. Add sausage, tasso, tomatoes with chiles, Slap Ya Mama Cajun Pepper Sauce, Slap Ya Mama Original Blend Cajun Seasoning, salt, and paprika; simmer for 10 minutes. Add chicken and broth; bring to a boil. Stir in rice; reduce heat to low. Cover and simmer for 30 minutes, stirring every 10 minutes. Stir in parsley and green onion. Serve immediately.

MAW MAW'S RED BEANS & RICE

MAKES 5 TO 6 SERVINGS

- 3 tablespoons margarine
- 1 large sweet onion, chopped (about 2 cups)
- ½ large green bell pepper, diced (about ½ cup)
- 1 pound cooked sausage, sliced or diced
- 1 (15.5-ounce) can red beans*, undrained
- 1 (8-ounce) can tomatoes with green chiles, undrained
- 1 cup medium-grain rice
- 1 cup water
- 2 teaspoons Slap Ya Mama Original Blend Cajun Seasoning

1. In a large saucepan, heat margarine over medium heat. Add onion and bell pepper; cook until translucent, about 7 minutes. Add sausage and all remaining ingredients; bring to a boil. Reduce heat to medium-low; cover and cook until all liquid has been absorbed, about 20 minutes. Serve immediately.

We used Blue Runner Creole Cream Style Red Beans. You may substitute black-eyed peas or any other bean of your choice.

THAT'S RIGHT, FOLKS. SQUIRRELS!
VILLE PLATTE'S SQUIRREL SEASON

Louisiana's woodlands and wetlands are prime for hunting white-tailed deer, duck, quail, and even alligator. This sportsman's paradise also hosts an annual squirrel season.

Louisiana is home to Eastern gray squirrels and the slightly larger red fox squirrels. And hunting them, according to TW, seems—well—pretty straightforward.

"If they're on the ground, you shoot 'em on the ground, and if they're in the trees, you shoot 'em in the trees," says TW. "Shoot 'em wherever you can shoot 'em is what it amounts to. But you're talking to the worst squirrel hunter in the world, and that's me."

Not being a sharpshooter never stopped TW from spending weekends in the fall with his sons and their friends at hunting camps around Bayou Chicot. In Ville Platte, opening weekend of squirrel season has always been a very big deal. The town actually closes the first Friday of October. The ladies go shopping in nearby cities like Baton Rouge and Lafayette while the men head out into the woods to fend for themselves.

"It used to be the young guys, the *harias* (ha-de-yas) doing what we do, but now, it's gotten so much more family-oriented with all the kids and grandkids," says TW.

Jack and Joe remember going out into the woods early on, following their father closely with their BB guns. It was their special bonding time.

"Joe Willy killed his first squirrel when he was 5 or 6 years old," says TW. "Different cultures have different ways to spend time with the kids, but this is how we do it. When you take the kids in the woods, you get kinda close because there is nothing else happening. It's quiet and peaceful. When you see them kill their first deer or their first squirrel, there is nothing like it. They're so excited."

The Walker boys hunted morning and afternoon for their daily limit of eight squirrels, but they always made it back to camp to watch the Louisiana State University football game, where they cheered on their Tigers, who reign supreme in Cajun Country.

"Growing up, I got to take little adventures with my father and brother," recalls Jack. "We got to be boys, get in trouble, and get dirty, and do things we normally didn't get to do at home. We didn't realize at the time just how special those father-son weekends were."

When it came to cooking squirrels, TW was a gourmet chef. To this day, he's known for his Squirrel Sauce Piquante. After he and the boys cleaned the squirrels, they threw the meat into a pot, and cooked it down into a peppery, tomatoey sauce. They poured the sauce over rice for the perfect warm, filling supper after a crisp fall day in the woods.

SQUIRREL SAUCE PIQUANTE

MAKES 6 TO 8 SERVINGS

Tradition and spending time with family take center stage in Cajun culture, and this spice-filled recipe holds special memories for the Walkers.

4	squirrels, cut into pieces (about 1½ pounds)
2	teaspoons Slap Ya Mama Original Blend Cajun Seasoning
1	teaspoon sugar
½	teaspoon garlic powder
2	tablespoons vegetable oil
1	(14.5-ounce) can stewed tomatoes, smashed
½	(8-ounce) can golden mushroom soup
2	large sweet onions, chopped (about 4 cups)
1	large green bell pepper, chopped (about 1 cup)
1	cup chopped green onion
1	cup chopped fresh parsley

Hot cooked rice, to serve

1. Sprinkle squirrel pieces with Slap Ya Mama Original Blend Cajun Seasoning, sugar, and garlic powder. Place in a large pan or bowl, and refrigerate for 12 hours.
2. In a large stockpot, heat oil over medium heat. Add squirrel; cook until vegetables are browned. Remove from pot. Add tomatoes, soup, onion, and bell pepper; cook until browned. Return squirrel to pot; continue browning. Add a little water, and continue browning until water is gone. Add water until it almost covers the squirrel, and cook until tender, about 2 hours and 30 minutes, adding green onion and parsley during final 30 minutes of cooking. (Younger squirrels don't take as long.) Serve over hot cooked rice.

Note: You can also brown ½ pound sausage with the squirrel.

MAW MAW'S FRIED CHICKEN

MAKES 6 TO 8 SERVINGS

No Southern gathering is truly complete without a serving dish full of fried chicken. And Maw Maw's Fried Chicken is sure to convince any nonbelievers.

Peanut oil, for frying
3   cups all-purpose flour
2½ teaspoons Slap Ya Mama Original Blend Cajun Seasoning, divided
1   fryer chicken, cut into pieces

1. In a 12-inch cast-iron skillet, pour oil to a depth of about ½ inch, and heat oil over medium heat until an instant-read thermometer registers 350°.
2. In a large bowl, stir together flour and 1 teaspoon Slap Ya Mama Original Blend Cajun Seasoning. Sprinkle chicken with 1 teaspoon Slap Ya Mama Original Blend Cajun Seasoning. Working in batches, dredge chicken in flour mixture, gently shaking off excess.
3. Working in batches, fry chicken until golden brown and a meat thermometer inserted in thickest portion registers 165°, 6 to 7 minutes per side. Remove chicken, and let drain on paper towels. Sprinkle with remaining ½ teaspoon Slap Ya Mama Original Blend Cajun Seasoning.

PASTALAYA

MAKES 6 SERVINGS

Slap Ya Mama Pastalaya is a unique take on the traditional Cajun jambalaya. With smoked sausage, spicy chicken, fresh shrimp, and pasta instead of rice, this dish will most definitely become a household favorite.

- ¾ pound boneless skinless chicken breasts, cut into 1-inch pieces
- 3 teaspoons Slap Ya Mama Original Blend Cajun Seasoning, divided
- 2 tablespoons olive oil
- ½ large sweet onion, thinly sliced
- ½ pound smoked sausage, sliced
- 1 large green bell pepper, thinly sliced
- 1 large jalapeño, thinly sliced
- 4 cloves garlic, minced
- 1 (14.5-ounce) can diced tomatoes, drained
- 1 (8-ounce) can tomato sauce
- 1 cup chicken broth
- ½ teaspoon dried oregano
- ½ teaspoon dried basil
- ½ teaspoon dried thyme
- ¾ pound large fresh shrimp, peeled and deveined
- ¼ cup chopped fresh parsley
- 1 (16-ounce) package penne pasta, cooked according to package directions and kept warm

Garnish: chopped fresh parsley

1. In a medium bowl, toss together chicken and 1½ teaspoons Slap Ya Mama Original Blend Cajun Seasoning.

2. In a large skillet, heat oil over medium-high heat. Add chicken; cook until browned on all sides. Add onion; cook until slightly softened. Add sausage, bell pepper, jalapeño, and garlic; cook, stirring frequently, for 5 minutes. Add tomatoes, tomato sauce, broth, oregano, basil, thyme, and remaining 1½ teaspoons Slap Ya Mama Original Blend Cajun Seasoning; bring to a light boil. Reduce heat to medium-low, and simmer for 15 minutes.

3. Add shrimp and parsley, stirring until combined. Cook for 4 minutes, making sure shrimp are submerged. Serve over hot cooked pasta. Garnish with parsley, if desired.

HOLIDAY HAM

MAKES 14 TO 16 SERVINGS

Bring some Louisiana Cajun flavor to your next holiday dinner with this special ham recipe. The Slap Ya Mama spices and Southern cola flavors will have you wanting more year-round.

- 1 (1-pound) bag Slap Ya Mama Cajun Seafood Boil
- 1 (8-pound) picnic ham
- ½ cup water
- 1 (12-ounce) can cola
- 2 teaspoons Slap Ya Mama Original Blend Cajun Seasoning

1. Fill a large stockpot halfway full with water, and pour in Slap Ya Mama Cajun Seafood Boil. Bring to a boil over medium-high heat, and place ham in pot. Boil for about 1 hour. Remove ham; let drain and cool.
2. Preheat oven to 400°.
3. Trim top skin from ham, leaving a little fat. In a crisscross pattern, slice top of ham about ¼ inch deep.
4. Pour ½ cup water in bottom of a roasting pan. Add ham; pour cola over ham. Sprinkle ham with Slap Ya Mama Original Blend Cajun Seasoning.
5. Bake for 30 minutes. Reduce oven temperature to 350°, and bake until there is a nice crisp on exterior of ham, about 30 minutes more. Serve immediately.

CAJUN ROASTED CHICKEN

MAKES 4 TO 6 SERVINGS

Nothing welcomes loved ones to your home like the smell of roasted chicken. Plenty of seasoning, garlic, and butter guarantees a tender and flavorful bird.

- 1 (4- to 5-pound) whole chicken
- 2 tablespoons olive oil
- 1 tablespoon Slap Ya Mama Original Blend Cajun Seasoning
- 1 lemon, cut in half
- 1 small onion, quartered
- ½ green bell pepper, sliced
- ¼ cup unsalted butter, cubed
- 3 to 4 cloves garlic, crushed
- ½ teaspoon dried thyme

1. Preheat oven to 350°.
2. Clean chicken of excess fat, and clear out cavity of chicken. Pat chicken dry. Coat entire chicken with oil, and rub outside and inside of chicken with Slap Ya Mama Original Blend Cajun Seasoning. Stuff lemon, onion, bell pepper, butter, garlic, and thyme into chicken cavity. Using butcher's twine, tie legs together tightly. Place in a shallow roasting pan or large cast-iron skillet.
3. Bake for 30 minutes, occasionally basting with juices from bottom of pan or skillet. Reduce oven temperature to 325°, and bake, occasionally basting with juices, until a meat thermometer inserted in thickest portion registers 165°, about 1 hour more.

MEATBALL STEW

MAKES 4 SERVINGS

Forget pasta—combine these beef-and-pork meatballs with warm broth and rice.

- 1 pound ground beef
- 1 pound ground pork
- 1 large sweet onion, chopped (about 2 cups) and divided
- 1 large green bell pepper, chopped (about 1 cup) and divided
- 2 teaspoons Slap Ya Mama Original Blend Cajun Seasoning, divided
- 1 large egg
- 2 tablespoons Worcestershire sauce
- ½ cup Dark Roux (recipe follows)
- 2 teaspoons minced garlic (about 2 cloves)
- ½ cup chopped green onion
- ½ cup chopped fresh parsley
- Hot cooked rice, to serve

1. In large bowl, combine beef, pork, and a small amount of onion and bell pepper. Sprinkle with 1 teaspoon Slap Ya Mama Original Blend Cajun Seasoning.

2. In a small bowl, whisk together egg and Worcestershire. Add egg mixture to meat mixture, and mix well with your hands. Shape mixture into 12 palm-size meatballs. Set aside.

3. Fill a 10-inch cast-iron stockpot or Dutch oven with 2 inches water. Bring to a boil; reduce heat to medium. Add Dark Roux; cook, stirring constantly, until melted. Reduce heat; add meatballs, garlic, remaining onion, remaining bell pepper, and water to just cover meatballs. Sprinkle with remaining 1 teaspoon Slap Ya Mama Original Blend Cajun Seasoning; stir carefully. Cook over medium heat, stirring occasionally, for about 1 hour and 30 minutes, adding green onion and parsley during final 10 minutes of cooking. Serve over hot cooked rice.

DARK ROUX

MAKES ABOUT 1½ CUP

- 1 cup vegetable oil
- 1 cup all-purpose flour

1. In an 8-quart stockpot, heat oil over medium heat for about 5 minutes; add flour, stirring to combine. Cook, stirring frequently, until a dark peanut butter-colored roux forms, about 20 minutes.

FRIED PORK CHOPS

MAKES 6 SERVINGS

Best served with heaping helpings of mashed potatoes and green beans, these bone-in chops are fried to perfection.

6   (½-inch-thick) bone-in center-cut pork chops
1½   tablespoons Slap Ya Mama Original Blend Cajun Seasoning, divided
2   cups whole buttermilk
3½   cups all-purpose flour
Vegetable oil or lard, for frying

1. Place pork chops on a large plate, and sprinkle both sides with ½ tablespoon Slap Ya Mama Original Blend Cajun Seasoning. Stack pork chops, and cover with plastic wrap. Refrigerate for at least 4 hours or up to 24 hours.
2. Place buttermilk in a shallow bowl. In another shallow bowl, combine flour and remaining 1 tablespoon Slap Ya Mama Original Blend Cajun Seasoning.
3. In a large Dutch oven, pour oil or lard to a depth of 4 inches, and heat over medium-high heat until a deep-fry thermometer registers 365°.
4. Dip pork chops in buttermilk, letting excess drip off. Dredge in flour mixture, shaking off excess. Working in batches, fry until golden brown, 4 to 5 minutes. Let drain on paper towels.

STUFFED WILD DUCK BREAST

MAKES 4 SERVINGS

Creamy jalapeño flavor stuffed into wild game and wrapped with bacon. You won't be able to eat just one.

- 2½ cups whole milk
- 4 boneless duck breasts, cleaned
- 1 (20-ounce) bottle cola
- 2 teaspoons Slap Ya Mama Original Blend Cajun Seasoning
- 2 teaspoons Slap Ya Mama Cajun Pepper Sauce
- 4 ounces cream cheese, softened
- 1 jalapeño, seeded and thinly sliced
- 8 slices thick-cut bacon
- Wooden picks, soaked in water for about 15 minutes
- Black Cherry Sauce (recipe follows)

1. Place milk in a large bowl. Add duck, and refrigerate for about 1 hour. Drain milk, and add cola. Refrigerate for 1 hour.

2. Remove duck from bowl; let drain, and pat dry with paper towels. Using a sharp knife, cut a small pocket lengthwise into each duck breast. (Be careful not to cut all the way through.) Place duck breasts in another bowl; sprinkle with Slap Ya Mama Original Blend Cajun Seasoning, and add Slap Ya Mama Cajun Pepper Sauce.

3. Preheat grill to medium heat (300° to 350°).

4. In a small bowl, stir together cream cheese and jalapeño. Be sure to cover all jalapeño slices with cream cheese. Place cream cheese-covered jalapeño slices into cut pockets of each duck breast.

5. For each breast, arrange 2 slices bacon side by side, and then roll duck breast and bacon together. To keep bacon wrapped around duck, secure with a wooden pick at end of each bacon slice.

6. Grill, turning occasionally, for 15 to 30 minutes, depending on thickness of duck breasts. Don't overcook them, as they will dry out. Remove wooden picks before serving. Drizzle Black Cherry Sauce over bacon-wrapped duck breasts, or use as a dipping sauce.

BLACK CHERRY SAUCE
MAKES ABOUT 1 CUP

- 2 cups pitted black cherries
- 1½ cups chicken broth
- 2 cloves garlic, minced
- 1 sprig fresh tarragon, finely chopped

1. In the container of a blender, place cherries; blend until slushy.

2. In a medium saucepan, bring cherries, broth, garlic, and tarragon to a boil over medium-high heat. Reduce heat to low, and simmer until thickened.

POT-ROASTED WHOLE DUCK

MAKES ABOUT 6 SERVINGS

Create a warm and inviting meal for your family with the rich smells and taste of roasted duck, perfect for any special gathering.

- 1 (5-pound) whole duck
- 2 teaspoons Slap Ya Mama Original Blend Cajun Seasoning
- 2 large sweet onions, quartered
- 4 stalks celery, halved
- 3 large green bell peppers, seeded and halved
- 4 heads garlic, halved
- 2 tablespoons firmly packed light brown sugar
- 1 tablespoon unsalted butter, melted

1. Preheat oven to 425°.
2. Using a sharp knife, prick skin of duck; sprinkle duck with Slap Ya Mama Original Blend Cajun Seasoning.
3. In a large oval Dutch oven, place onion, celery, bell pepper, and garlic in an even layer; place duck on top.
4. Bake until skin is light golden brown, about 40 minutes. Reduce oven temperature to 400°, and bake until a meat thermometer inserted in thickest portion registers 170°, about 50 minutes more.
5. Meanwhile, in a small bowl, stir together brown sugar and melted butter until smooth. Brush over duck skin during final 10 minutes of cooking. Let stand for 15 minutes before slicing.

VENISON SAUCE PIQUANTE

MAKES 8 TO 10 SERVINGS

A day of hunting with the Walkers means spending time with the family and bringing home plenty of fresh venison to share!

- 3 pounds venison shank, cut into 1-inch pieces
- 1½ teaspoons Slap Ya Mama Original Blend Cajun Seasoning
- 1 teaspoon sugar
- ½ teaspoon garlic powder
- 1 tablespoon vegetable oil
- 1 (8-ounce) can tomatoes with green chiles
- 1 (6-ounce) can mushroom steak sauce
- 2 large sweet onions, chopped (about 4 cups)
- 1 large green bell pepper, chopped (about 1 cup)
- 1 cup chopped green onion
- 1 cup chopped fresh parsley
- Hot cooked rice, to serve

1. Soak venison in hot water for 10 minutes. Squeeze all water and blood out of venison. Sprinkle with Slap Ya Mama Original Blend Cajun Seasoning, sugar, and garlic powder. Place in a large bowl or pan, and refrigerate overnight.

2. In a large stockpot, heat oil over medium heat. Add venison; cook until browned. Remove from pot. Add tomatoes with green chiles, mushroom steak sauce, onion, and bell pepper; cook until browned. Return venison to pot; continue browning. Add a little water, and continue browning until water is gone. Add water until just covering venison, and cook until tender, about 2 hours and 30 minutes, adding green onion and parsley during final 30 minutes of cooking. (Younger deer will not take as long.) Serve over hot cooked rice.

Note: You can also brown a pound of sausage with venison.

COOKING TIP FROM MAMA JEN

When browning your meat for a sauce, always stick it and lift it twice before adding your water for cooking. This means seasoning your meat, adding oil to your pot, and heating it up. Add meat to the pot and let it stick to the bottom and stir it up every so often. Once it sticks and leaves gratin (the brown bits that are also called fond), you add a little water and scrape the bottom to lift the gratin, let the water boil out, and let it stick again. This is when you add your onion, bell pepper, and garlic, and let them brown. Once you're done, add all the water you need to cook and then stir and lift the gratin. Then, you are ready to proceed.

PORK CHOP STEW

MAKES 6 SERVINGS

Cooked with vegetables and seasonings, this hearty stew is a fresh way to serve pork chops.

- 1 tablespoon Slap Ya Mama Original Blend Cajun Seasoning
- 6 (1-inch-thick) bone-in pork loin chops
- ½ cup Dark Roux (recipe on page 179)
- 3 cups water
- 1 medium red bell pepper, chopped
- 1 medium yellow onion, chopped
- 1 clove garlic, minced
- ½ teaspoon Slap Ya Mama Hot Blend Cajun Seasoning
- ¾ cup chopped green onion
- ¾ cup minced fresh parsley

Hot cooked rice, to serve

Garnish: chopped green onion, minced fresh parsley

1. Sprinkle Slap Ya Mama Original Blend Cajun Seasoning over both sides of pork chops; set aside.

2. In a Dutch oven, whisk together Dark Roux and 3 cups water until blended. Add bell pepper, onion, garlic, and Slap Ya Mama Hot Blend Cajun Seasoning; bring to a boil. Reduce heat, and simmer until vegetables are softened, about 5 minutes.

3. Add pork chops; bring to a boil. Reduce heat; cover and simmer for 15 minutes. Rotate chops. Add green onion and parsley; cover and cook until a meat thermometer inserted in pork registers 145°, 3 to 5 minutes. Let stand for 5 minutes. Serve over hot cooked rice. Garnish with green onion and parsley, if desired.

CAJUN FRIED TURKEY

MAKES 10 TO 14 SERVINGS

If you've never tried frying a turkey, what are you waiting for? Get ready for perfectly crispy skin and classic Cajun flavors.

- 1 (5-ounce) bottle Slap Ya Mama Cajun Pepper Sauce
- ¼ cup unsalted butter
- Juice of 2 lemons
- 1 tablespoon Slap Ya Mama Hot Blend Cajun Seasoning
- 1 (12- to 16-pound) turkey
- 5 gallons peanut oil

1. In a medium saucepan, heat Slap Ya Mama Cajun Pepper Sauce, butter, lemon juice, and Slap Ya Mama Hot Blend Cajun Seasoning over low heat until butter is melted. Using a large syringe, inject marinade into all meaty areas of turkey (breasts, thighs, legs, and wings). If possible, let turkey marinate for 2 to 4 hours in refrigerator. Remove turkey at least 30 minutes before frying.

2. Prepare turkey fryer according to manufacturer's instructions. Fill fryer stockpot with peanut oil to within 10 to 12 inches of top. Heat over medium-high heat until a deep-fry thermometer registers 300°. Lower turkey very slowly and carefully into pot, and cover. Maintain a temperature of 280° to 310°. Fry for 3½ minutes per pound of turkey; the internal temperature should be 165°. (For a 12-pound turkey, fry for approximately 42 minutes.) Remove turkey from pot, and let drain. Wrap in foil, and let stand for at least 15 minutes before carving.

COOKING TIP FROM MAMA JEN

If you can skin it or pluck it, you can "slap it" and eat it!

GRILLED PORK RIBS

MAKES 10 TO 12 SERVINGS

This is the perfect meal for a day of watching football and laughing over family stories. Fire up the grill and pass the napkins for this favorite.

3	(5-pound) racks spare pork ribs, membranes removed
3	tablespoons Slap Ya Mama Original Blend Cajun Seasoning
½	cup bourbon*
⅓	cup honey
¼	cup ketchup
3	tablespoons Worcestershire sauce
3	tablespoons apple cider vinegar
2	tablespoons Dijon mustard
1	tablespoon cane syrup
1	tablespoon Slap Ya Mama Cajun Hot Sauce

1. Sprinkle ribs with Slap Ya Mama Original Blend Cajun Seasoning, and cover with plastic wrap. Refrigerate for at least 8 hours or overnight. Let stand at room temperature for 30 minutes.

2. Preheat charcoal grill/smoker to 250°, adding charcoal and hickory chips as needed for heat and smoke.

3. In a medium saucepan, bring bourbon, honey, ketchup, Worcestershire, vinegar, mustard, cane syrup, and Slap Ya Mama Cajun Hot Sauce to a boil over medium-high heat. Reduce heat to medium; cook, stirring occasionally, until thickened, about 30 minutes. Cover and refrigerate until ready to use.

4. Add ribs to grill, meat side up, in an even layer. Cook for 3 to 3 hours and 30 minutes, basting with barbecue sauce every 30 minutes. Let stand for 10 minutes before serving. Serve with additional barbecue sauce.

*You can substitute ⅓ cup water and 2 tablespoons vanilla extract for bourbon, if desired.

CHICKEN GUMBO CASSEROLE

MAKES 12 TO 16 SERVINGS

Gumbo is a family staple, but it can be a lot of work. An easy casserole full of great gumbo flavor is perfect for a family dinner during the week.

- ¼ cup olive oil
- 1 pound tasso, diced
- 2 cups chopped yellow onion
- 1 cup chopped celery
- ½ cup chopped red bell pepper
- ½ cup chopped green bell pepper
- 2 cups long-grain white rice
- 1 quart chicken broth
- 2 (14.5-ounce) cans fire-roasted diced tomatoes
- 2 cups chopped cooked chicken
- 2 cups fresh or frozen sliced okra, thawed
- 2 tablespoons Slap Ya Mama Cajun Hot Sauce
- 1½ tablespoons Worcestershire sauce
- 2 teaspoons Slap Ya Mama Low Sodium Cajun Seasoning
- 1½ teaspoons garlic powder

Garnish: chopped green onion, chopped fresh parsley

1. Preheat oven to 350°. Spray a 4-quart baking dish with nonstick cooking spray. Set aside.
2. In a large Dutch oven, heat olive oil over medium-high heat. Add tasso, onion, celery, and bell peppers. Cook, stirring frequently, until tasso is lightly browned and vegetables are softened, about 10 minutes. Add rice; cook, stirring constantly, 2 minutes. Add broth and tomatoes; bring to a boil. Reduce heat to medium-low, and cook, covered, until rice is tender, 18 to 20 minutes. Remove from heat.
3. Add cooked chicken, okra, Slap Ya Mama Cajun Hot Sauce, Worcestershire, Slap Ya Mama Low Sodium Cajun Seasoning, and garlic powder, stirring to combine. Spoon mixture into prepared dish, and cover with aluminum foil.
4. Bake until liquid is absorbed and okra is tender, about 20 minutes. Garnish with green onion and parsley, if desired.

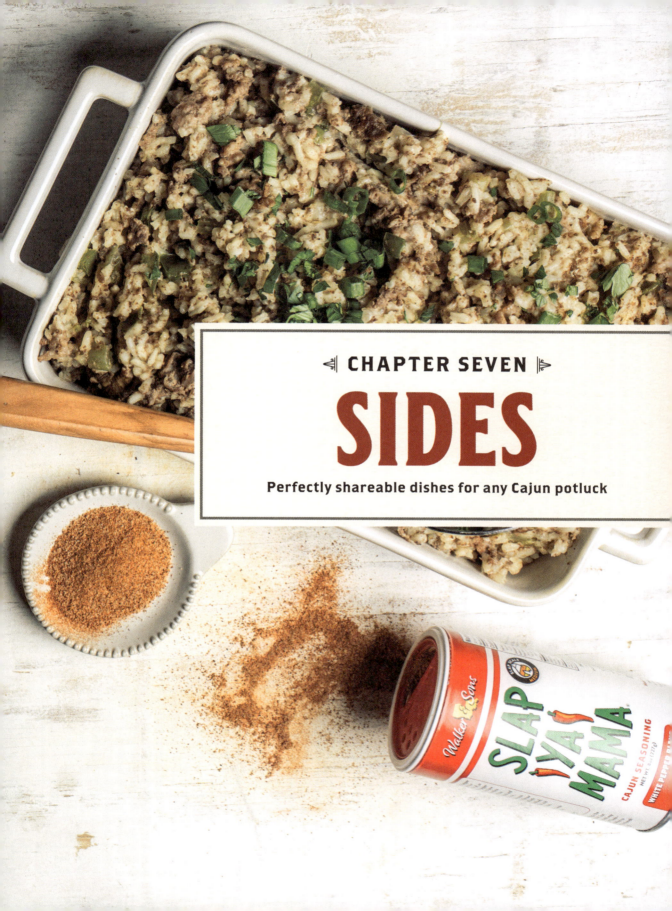

CHAPTER SEVEN

SIDES

Perfectly shareable dishes for any Cajun potluck

WORLD-FAMOUS SLAP YA MAMA ATOMIC POTATOES

MAKES 4 SERVINGS

Life's too short to eat bland mashed potatoes. Turn up the heat and throw a little spice into these spuds.

- 3 pounds russet potatoes
- 1 tablespoon canola oil
- Slap Ya Mama Original Blend Cajun Seasoning, to taste
- 1 large yellow onion, chopped
- 1 large green bell pepper, chopped
- ½ teaspoon minced garlic (optional)
- Garnish: sliced jalapeño

1. Peel potatoes, and cut into bite-size pieces.
2. Cover bottom of a large stockpot with oil, and heat over high heat. Add potatoes, and stir until coated with oil. Season with Slap Ya Mama Original Blend Cajun Seasoning, to taste, and begin to brown potatoes, stirring occasionally.
3. Continue to stir while adding onion, bell pepper, and garlic (if desired). Fill pot with water until it reaches top of potatoes. Bring to a full boil, and stir occasionally from top of pot to bottom.
4. When potatoes begin to break down, reduce heat to a slow boil, and stir frequently to prevent sticking. Continue with a slow boil until potatoes have a thick, chunky consistency. Once this consistency is reached, remove from heat, and let stand while stirring occasionally for 10 to 15 minutes before serving. Garnish with jalapeño and additional Slap Ya Mama Original Blend Cajun Seasoning.

DIRTY RICE DRESSING & CORNBREAD DRESSING

Rice or cornbread—it'll be a tough choice once you try these two classic recipes.

DIRTY RICE DRESSING
MAKES 8 SERVINGS

- 1 pound chicken livers
- 1 pound chicken gizzards
- 1 tablespoon canola oil
- 1 pound lean ground pork
- 1 tablespoon unsalted butter
- 2 cups chopped onion
- 1½ cups finely chopped celery
- 1 cup chopped bell pepper
- 5 cloves garlic, minced
- 5 cups chicken broth, divided
- 2 teaspoons kosher salt
- 2 cups long-grain rice
- 1 teaspoon Slap Ya Mama White Pepper Blend Seasoning
- ¼ teaspoon Slap Ya Mama Hot Blend Cajun Seasoning
- Garnish: sliced green onion, chopped fresh parsley

1. In the work bowl of a food processor, place chicken livers and gizzards; pulse until ground.
2. Heat oil in a large Dutch oven over medium heat. Add liver mixture and pork; cook until browned. Pour off excess oil, and add butter. Add onion, celery, bell pepper, and garlic; cook for 5 minutes. Add 1 cup broth; cover and simmer for 5 minutes. Uncover and cook until broth is evaporated. Add salt and remaining 4 cups broth; bring to a boil over high heat. Add rice; stir, and return to a boil. Cover and simmer for 15 minutes.
3. Fold rice mixture from bottom to top. Cover and cook until rice is tender and liquid is absorbed, 5 to 10 minutes. Sprinkle with Slap Ya Mama White Pepper Blend Seasoning and Slap Ya Mama Hot Blend Cajun Seasoning. Serve hot. Garnish with green onion and parsley, if desired.

CORNBREAD DRESSING
MAKES 8 SERVINGS

- 1 cup unsalted butter, divided
- 3 cups whole buttermilk
- 8 large eggs, divided
- 3 cups plain yellow cornmeal
- 1 cup all-purpose flour
- 2 tablespoons sugar
- 4 teaspoons kosher salt, divided
- 2 teaspoons baking powder
- 1 teaspoon Slap Ya Mama Hot Blend Cajun Seasoning
- 1 teaspoon Slap Ya Mama Original Blend Cajun Seasoning
- 1 teaspoon baking soda
- 3 cups sliced celery
- 2 cups chopped yellow onion
- 2 cloves garlic, minced
- 1 (32-ounce) carton chicken broth
- 1 cup toasted pecans, chopped
- 4 teaspoons poultry seasoning
- 1 tablespoon fresh thyme leaves
- ½ teaspoon Slap Ya Mama White Pepper Blend Seasoning
- ½ teaspoon ground black pepper

1. Preheat oven to 425°.
2. In a 12-inch cast-iron skillet, melt ½ cup butter over medium-high heat. Pour butter into a medium bowl; whisk in buttermilk and 3 eggs. Place skillet in oven to preheat.
3. In a large bowl, whisk together cornmeal, flour, sugar, 2 teaspoons salt, baking powder, Slap Ya Mama Hot Blend Cajun Seasoning, Slap Ya Mama Original Blend Cajun Seasoning, and baking soda. Pour buttermilk mixture into cornmeal mixture; stir until combined. Carefully pour batter into hot skillet.
4. Bake until a wooden pick inserted in center comes out clean, 20 to 25 minutes. Invert cornbread onto a wire rack. Let cool; crumble. Reduce oven temperature to 375°.
5. Wipe skillet clean. Add remaining ½ cup butter to skillet; melt over medium-high heat. Add celery, onion, and garlic; cook, stirring occasionally, until softened, about 5 minutes. Remove from heat.
6. In a large bowl, whisk together broth and remaining 5 eggs. Gently stir in crumbled cornbread, celery mixture, pecans, poultry seasoning, thyme, Slap Ya Mama White Pepper Blend Seasoning, black pepper, and remaining 2 teaspoons salt. Spoon cornbread mixture back into skillet.
7. Bake until top is golden brown and dressing is firm to the touch, 45 to 50 minutes.

CANDIED YAMS & PECANS

MAKES 8 TO 10 SERVINGS

It's not a family gathering until someone brings the candied yams. There won't be any leftovers from this dish.

- 3 pounds sweet potatoes, peeled and cut into 1½-inch chunks
- 4 cups apple cider
- 2 cups water
- ½ cup granulated sugar
- ¼ cup firmly packed light brown sugar
- 2 tablespoons unsalted butter, melted
- 1 tablespoon Kiss Ya Mama Cinnamon Sugar
- 1 teaspoon Slap Ya Mama Hot Blend Cajun Seasoning
- ½ teaspoon orange zest
- ¼ teaspoon kosher salt
- 2 large eggs
- 4 cups miniature marshmallows

Candied Pecans (recipe follows)

1. Preheat oven to 350°. Spray a 13x9-inch baking dish with cooking spray.
2. In a medium Dutch oven, bring sweet potatoes, apple cider, and 2 cups water to a boil over medium-high heat. Reduce heat, and simmer until tender, 15 to 17 minutes. Drain, reserving ⅓ cup cooking liquid.
3. In a large bowl, place sweet potatoes, reserved ⅓ cup cooking liquid, sugars, melted butter, Kiss Ya Mama Cinnamon Sugar, Slap Ya Mama Hot Blend Cajun Seasoning, zest, and salt. Using a potato masher, mash to desired consistency. Stir in eggs. Spoon into prepared pan, spreading evenly. Cover with foil.
4. Bake for 30 minutes. Uncover and bake for 10 minutes more. Sprinkle with marshmallows and Candied Pecans. Bake until marshmallows are lightly browned, about 7 minutes more.

CANDIED PECANS

MAKES 1½ CUPS

- 6 tablespoons firmly packed light brown sugar
- 3 tablespoons unsalted butter
- 1 teaspoon Kiss Ya Mama Cinnamon Sugar
- ¼ teaspoon Slap Ya Mama Hot Blend Cajun Seasoning
- ⅛ teaspoon kosher salt
- 1½ cups pecan halves, toasted

1. Line a small baking sheet with foil; spray with cooking spray.
2. In a medium skillet, combine brown sugar, butter, Kiss Ya Mama Cinnamon Sugar, Slap Ya Mama Hot Blend Cajun Seasoning, and salt. Cook over medium heat, stirring occasionally, until butter is melted and sugar is moistened. Add pecans, stirring until coated. Spoon mixture onto prepared pan. Let stand until completely cool. Break into pieces.

CRAWFISH MAC & CHEESE

MAKES 15 SERVINGS

Crawfish, macaroni, and six different types of cheeses are baked together in this irresistible family favorite.

- 1 (16-ounce) package elbow macaroni, cooked according to package directions
- 2 tablespoons unsalted butter
- ½ (16-ounce) package cooked crawfish tails
- 1 (8-ounce) jar pimientos, drained
- 2 cups shredded mozzarella cheese
- 2 cups shredded sharp Cheddar cheese
- 1 cup shredded Parmesan cheese
- 1 cup shredded Gruyère cheese
- 1 cup shredded Gouda cheese
- 1 cup shredded fontina cheese
- 1 cup whole milk
- 3 large eggs, lightly beaten
- 2 teaspoons Slap Ya Mama Original Blend Cajun Seasoning
- 1 teaspoon kosher salt
- ½ teaspoon ground black pepper
- ¼ teaspoon garlic powder
- ⅛ teaspoon cayenne pepper
- ⅛ teaspoon Slap Ya Mama Hot Blend Cajun Seasoning
- 1 cup crushed buttery round crackers

1. Preheat oven to 350°. Spray 15 (1-cup) gratin dishes with cooking spray.
2. In a large bowl, stir together cooked pasta and butter until butter is melted. Add crawfish, pimientos, cheeses, milk, eggs, Slap Ya Mama Original Blend Cajun Seasoning, salt, black pepper, garlic powder, cayenne, and Slap Ya Mama Hot Blend Cajun Seasoning. Divide macaroni mixture among prepared dishes, and smooth tops with a spoon.
3. Bake for 10 minutes. Top each portion with crushed crackers, and bake until edges are bubbly, about 5 minutes more. Serve immediately.

Note: If you don't have individual dishes, bake this cheesy crowd-pleaser in a 4-quart baking dish.

COOKING TIP FROM MAMA JEN

When boiling pasta, you can check if it's done by throwing a noodle at the refrigerator. If it sticks, it is done.

ROASTED BRUSSELS SPROUTS

MAKES 4 SERVINGS

Beautifully roasted Brussels sprouts with an incredible dressing makes this the perfect side dish to any meal.

- 1 pound Brussels sprouts, trimmed and halved
- ½ red onion, sliced
- 1 tablespoon olive oil
- 1½ teaspoons Slap Ya Mama Low Sodium Cajun Seasoning
- 1½ tablespoons balsamic vinegar
- 2 teaspoons honey
- 1½ teaspoons Creole mustard

1. Preheat oven to 425°.
2. In a large bowl, stir together Brussels sprouts, onion, oil, and Slap Ya Mama Low Sodium Cajun Seasoning. Spread into an ovenproof skillet or rimmed baking pan.
3. Bake until tender and lightly browned, 25 to 30 minutes, stirring halfway through baking.
4. In a small bowl, stir together vinegar, honey, and mustard. Drizzle over roasted Brussels sprouts, and gently stir. Serve immediately.

COOKING TIP FROM MAMA JEN

Always taste your food before serving it to be sure it is seasoned to your liking.

GREEN BEAN CASSEROLE

MAKES 8 SERVINGS

Break out the french-fried onions. Your holiday table will love the amped-up flavor the Slap Ya Mama seasonings bring to this casserole.

2	pounds fresh green beans, rinsed, trimmed, and halved
4	slices bacon, chopped into ¼-inch pieces
½	large onion, chopped
2	cloves garlic, minced
¼	cup unsalted butter
¼	cup all-purpose flour
2½	cups whole milk
½	cup half-and-half
1	cup grated sharp Cheddar cheese
1½	teaspoons Slap Ya Mama Original Blend Cajun Seasoning
1	teaspoon light brown sugar
½	teaspoon Slap Ya Mama Hot Blend Cajun Seasoning
1	(4-ounce) jar sliced pimientos, drained
1	cup french-fried onions

1. Fill a large stockpot halfway full with water, add a dash of salt, and bring to a light boil. Add green beans, and boil for 3 to 4 minutes. Using a slotted spoon, remove beans from boiling water, and immediately drop into a large bowl of ice water. Once beans have cooled, drain and set aside.
2. Preheat oven to 350°.
3. In a large skillet, cook bacon over medium heat for 2 minutes. Add onion and garlic; cook until bacon is done and onion is translucent, 3 to 5 minutes. Remove from heat, and set aside.
4. In a large skillet, melt butter over medium heat. Sprinkle in flour, stir well, and cook for 2 minutes. Add milk and half-and-half; cook, stirring constantly, until sauce thickens, about 5 minutes. Add cheese, Slap Ya Mama Original Blend Cajun Seasoning, brown sugar, and Slap Ya Mama Hot Blend Cajun Seasoning; cook, stirring constantly, until cheese is melted. Remove from heat; add pimientos and bacon mixture, stirring well.
5. In a 1½-quart baking dish, combine green beans and sauce mixture. Stir well, and spread evenly across dish. Top with french-fried onions.
6. Bake for 30 minutes. Serve immediately.

CLASSIC COLLARD GREENS

MAKES 8 SERVINGS

Bacon drippings and smoked turkey turn these greens into a side that can stand on its own.

- 2 tablespoons bacon drippings
- 2 cups chopped sweet onion
- 4 bunches collard greens, stemmed and chopped (about 32 cups)
- 1 smoked turkey leg
- 2 cups low-sodium chicken broth
- 2 teaspoons kosher salt
- ½ teaspoon Slap Ya Mama Hot Blend Cajun Seasoning
- ¼ cup apple cider vinegar

1. In a large Dutch oven, heat bacon drippings over medium-high heat. Add onion; cook, stirring occasionally, until onion is softened, about 8 minutes. Add collards in batches, stirring until wilted after each addition. Add turkey leg, broth, salt, and Slap Ya Mama Hot Blend Cajun Seasoning; cover and cook until greens are tender, about 25 minutes. Stir in vinegar. Serve immediately.

COOKING TIP FROM MAMA JEN

Add uncooked rice to your saltshaker so the salt doesn't harden and clump.

PARMESAN GRILLED CORN

MAKES 4 SERVINGS

Parmesan-coated grilled corn spiced up with Slap Ya Mama Original Blend Cajun Seasoning is the perfect addition to any barbecue.

- ½   cup shredded Parmesan cheese, divided
- ¼   cup unsalted butter, melted
- 1   tablespoon Slap Ya Mama Original Blend Cajun Seasoning
- ½   teaspoon dried thyme
- 4   ears fresh corn, shucked
- 1   tablespoon chopped fresh parsley

1. Preheat grill to medium-high heat (350° to 400°).
2. In a small bowl, combine ¼ cup Parmesan, melted butter, Slap Ya Mama Original Blend Cajun Seasoning, and thyme; set aside.
3. Using a large sheet of foil, create a tray for corncobs to sit in. Lay corn inside foil tray. Coat corn with butter mixture, making sure corn is entirely covered. Using foil tray and more foil, tightly wrap corn into a foil pack, making sure there are no holes in foil pack.
4. Place foil pack on grill, and cook for 35 to 40 minutes. Carefully open foil pack. Sprinkle with remaining ¼ cup Parmesan. Top with parsley. Serve immediately.

ROASTED ASPARAGUS WITH CAJUN PECANS

MAKES 6 SERVINGS

The garlic snap of asparagus pairs with the Creole crunch of pecans in our go-to vegetable dish.

- 2 pounds fresh asparagus, trimmed
- 2 tablespoons vegetable oil
- ¾ teaspoon Slap Ya Mama Signature Seasoning Garlic Salt
- ¼ teaspoon ground black pepper
- Garnish: Cajun Pecans (recipe follows)

1. Preheat oven to broil.
2. On a rimmed baking sheet, place asparagus. Drizzle with oil, and sprinkle with Slap Ya Mama Signature Seasoning Garlic Salt and pepper. Using tongs, toss to coat.
3. Broil, turning occasionally, until golden brown and tender, 8 to 10 minutes. Transfer to a serving platter, and garnish with Cajun Pecans, if desired.

CAJUN PECANS
MAKES 2 CUPS

- ½ cup unsalted butter, melted
- 2 teaspoons Slap Ya Mama Hot Blend Cajun Seasoning
- 1 teaspoon Slap Ya Mama Signature Blend Garlic Salt
- 1 teaspoon Worcestershire sauce
- ¼ teaspoon kosher salt
- ¼ teaspoon ground black pepper
- 2 cups pecan halves

1. Preheat oven to 325°. Line a rimmed baking sheet with parchment paper.
2. In a large bowl, stir together melted butter, Slap Ya Mama Hot Blend Cajun Seasoning, Slap Ya Mama Signature Blend Garlic Salt, Worcestershire, kosher salt, and pepper. Add pecans, and stir until coated. Spread in an even layer on prepared pan.
3. Bake until toasted, about 30 to 40 minutes, stirring every 10 minutes. Let cool completely on pan. Store in an airtight container for up to 1 week.

FIELD PEA CAVIAR

MAKES 8 TO 10 SERVINGS

Full of colorful, fresh produce, this dish is great with chips or fresh veggies during the summer.

½	pound dried field peas, cooked
2	cups fresh multicolored corn kernels (about 3 ears)
½	cup diced red onion
½	cup diced red bell pepper
½	cup diced green bell pepper
½	cup chopped fresh green onion
¼	cup diced seeded jalapeño
¼	cup chopped fresh cilantro
1½	teaspoons lime zest
¼	cup fresh lime juice
¼	cup olive oil
2	teaspoons Slap Ya Mama Original Blend Cajun Seasoning

Pita chips and sliced cucumbers, to serve

1. In a large bowl, stir together cooked peas, corn, onion, bell peppers, green onion, jalapeño, cilantro, lime zest and juice, oil, and Slap Ya Mama Original Blend Cajun Seasoning until combined. Cover and refrigerate for at least 1 hour before serving. Serve with pita chips and cucumbers.

CORN TASSO MAQUE CHOUX

MAKES 6 SERVINGS

Sweet yellow corn and spicy, smoked tasso ham makes for a delicious dish, great on it's own for a light lunch or paired with a tasty main.

- 3 tablespoons olive oil, divided
- 6 ounces tasso ham, diced (about 1 cup)
- 1 cup chopped orange bell pepper
- 1 poblano pepper, diced
- ¾ cup chopped sweet onion
- ½ cup chopped celery
- 1 jalapeño, diced
- 4 cups fresh corn kernels (about 6 ears)
- 1½ teaspoons minced garlic
- 1 cup heavy whipping cream
- 1 tablespoon chopped fresh parsley
- 1 tablespoon chopped fresh oregano
- 1¼ teaspoons kosher salt
- ½ teaspoon ground black pepper
- ½ teaspoon Slap Ya Mama Original Blend Cajun Seasoning
- 1½ cups cherry tomatoes, halved

Garnish: chopped fresh oregano

1. In a large cast-iron skillet, heat 2 tablespoons oil over medium-low heat. Add tasso, and cook, stirring frequently, until browned, 8 to 9 minutes. Using a slotted spoon, remove tasso from skillet, and let drain on paper towels.
2. In same skillet, add remaining 1 tablespoon oil, and increase heat to medium. Add bell pepper, poblano pepper, onion, celery, and jalapeño; cook, stirring frequently, until crisp-tender, 5 to 6 minutes. Stir in corn and garlic; cook, stirring frequently, until fragrant and corn is tender, 2 to 3 minutes. Add cooked tasso, cream, parsley, oregano, salt, black pepper, and Slap Ya Mama Original Blend Cajun Seasoning, stirring until well combined. Reduce heat to medium-low, and cook, stirring frequently, until cream is slightly reduced, about 8 minutes. Stir in tomatoes, and cook until just tender and heated through, 4 to 5 minutes. Garnish with oregano, if desired. Serve warm.

BLACK-EYED PEAS AND SAUSAGE

MAKES 10 TO 12 SERVINGS

Our family can't ring in the New Year without a big bowl of black-eyed peas. This recipe is one of our favorites. It's guaranteed to bring you luck and prosperity all year long.

1	pound smoked sausage, sliced into ¼-inch rounds
1	cup diced yellow onion
1	cup diced red bell pepper
1	cup diced green bell pepper
4	cloves garlic, grated
1	(1-pound) bag dried black-eyed peas, rinsed and drained
1	(32-ounce) container low-sodium chicken broth
2	cups water
2	dried bay leaves
2	tablespoons red wine vinegar
1	teaspoon Slap Ya Mama Original Blend Cajun Seasoning

1. In a heavy-duty resealable plastic bag, add sausage, onion, bell peppers, and garlic. Freeze until ready to use or for up to 6 months.

2. In a 7-quart slow cooker, add frozen sausage mixture, peas, broth, 2 cups water, and bay leaves. Cover and cook on high until peas are tender, 5 to 6 hours. Stir in vinegar and Slap Ya Mama Original Blend Cajun Seasoning. Store, refrigerated, for up to 5 days.

LOUISIANA OYSTER DRESSING

MAKES 6 TO 8 SERVINGS

A holiday dinner isn't complete without a big batch of oyster dressing. While we love to use freshly shucked oysters in ours, you can always grab a container of pre-shucked oysters from your local seafood market or grocery store.

- ¼ cup unsalted butter
- ¼ pound smoked andouille sausage, chopped
- 1 cup chopped celery
- 1 cup chopped yellow onion
- 1 cup chopped green bell pepper
- 4 cloves garlic, minced
- 2 (8-ounce) containers shucked oysters, drained, ½ cup liquid reserved, and large oysters quartered
- ¼ cup vegetable broth
- 1 tablespoon fresh lemon juice
- 1¾ teaspoons Slap Ya Mama Original Blend Cajun Seasoning
- 8 cups 1-inch cubed day-old or toasted French bread
- ¼ cup Italian-seasoned bread crumbs
- 2 tablespoons chopped fresh parsley
- 4 teaspoons fresh thyme leaves
- 2 tablespoons unsalted butter, melted

Garnish: chopped fresh parsley

1. Preheat oven to 325°.
2. In a 10-inch cast-iron skillet, melt ¼ cup butter over medium-high heat. Add sausage; cook until browned, 4 to 5 minutes. Transfer sausage to a large bowl using a slotted spoon, reserving drippings in skillet. Reduce heat to medium.
3. Add celery, onion, bell pepper, and garlic to drippings in skillet; cook until softened, 4 to 5 minutes. Transfer celery mixture to bowl with sausage.
4. In a large bowl, whisk together ½ cup reserved oyster liquid, broth, lemon juice, and Slap Ya Mama Original Blend Cajun Seasoning. (If oyster liquid doesn't measure ½ cup, add vegetable broth as needed.) Gently stir in sausage mixture, oysters, bread cubes, bread crumbs, parsley, and thyme until well combined. Spoon mixture back into skillet. Loosely cover with foil.
5. Bake for 35 minutes. Uncover and drizzle with 2 tablespoons melted butter. Bake until bread is lightly browned, about 15 minutes. Let stand for 10 minutes before serving. Garnish with parsley, if desired.

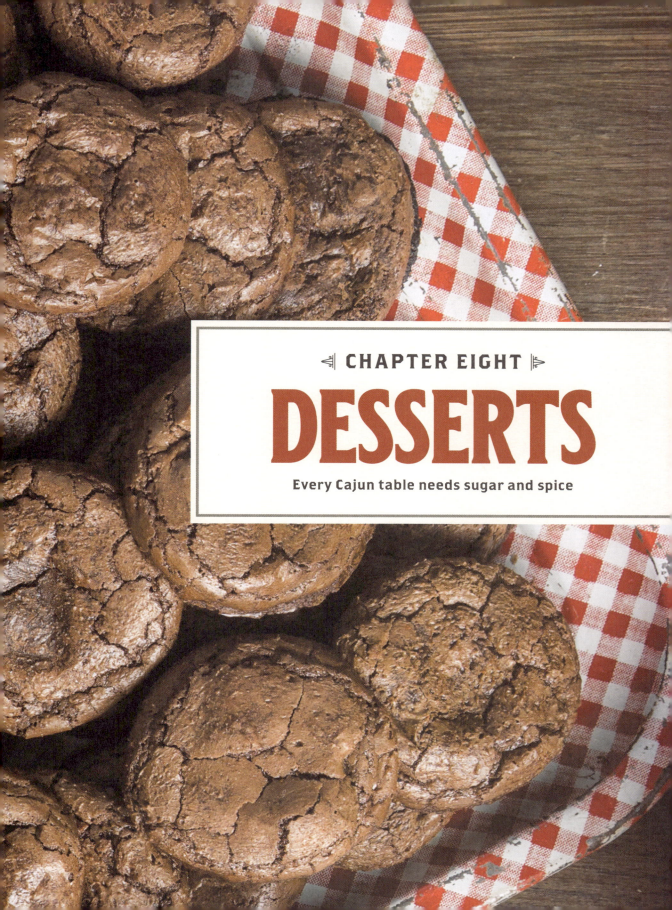

CHAPTER EIGHT
DESSERTS
Every Cajun table needs sugar and spice

MAW MAW'S PECAN PIE

MAKES 1 (9-INCH) PIE

This family favorite, and Maw Maw's most famous recipe, is served up at every Walker holiday dinner and family gathering. After you give it a try, it just might become one of your family's most requested recipes, too.

- ½ (14.1-ounce) package refrigerated piecrusts
- 1 cup granulated sugar
- ½ cup dark corn syrup
- ¼ cup unsalted butter, melted
- 3 large eggs, lightly beaten
- 1 cup chopped pecans

1. Preheat oven to 350°.
2. On a lightly floured surface, roll piecrust into a 12-inch circle. Transfer to a 9-inch pie plate, pressing into bottom and up sides. Fold edges under, and crimp as desired. Prick bottom of dough a few times with a fork.
3. Bake for 10 minutes. Leave oven on.
4. In a large bowl, whisk together sugar, corn syrup, melted butter, and eggs. Stir in pecans. Pour into prepared crust.
5. Bake until edges are set and center is slightly jiggly, 45 to 55 minutes.

COOKING TIP FROM MAMA JEN

When prebaking a piecrust, always prick the bottom of the crust several times with a fork before baking so that it does not bubble up.

BREAD PUDDING

MAKES 8 SERVINGS

Hearty and classic, this meringue-topped beauty is meant for passing around a table filled with loved ones.

- 8 large eggs, separated
- 2⅔ cups plus ½ cup granulated sugar, divided
- 3 (12-ounce) cans evaporated milk
- ½ cup unsalted butter, melted
- 2 tablespoons bourbon
- 1 tablespoon plus ½ teaspoon vanilla extract, divided
- 1 teaspoon Slap Ya Mama Original Blend Cajun Seasoning
- 1½ (16-ounce) loaves French bread, cut into 1-inch cubes
- ½ teaspoon almond extract

1. Preheat oven to 350°. Spray a 3-quart baking dish with cooking spray.
2. In a large bowl, whisk egg yolks, and 2⅔ cups sugar, whisking until thick and pale yellow. Whisk in evaporated milk, melted butter, bourbon, 1 tablespoon vanilla, and Slap Ya Mama Original Blend Cajun Seasoning until smooth. Fold in bread cubes until coated. Spoon into prepared baking dish.
3. Bake until a knife inserted in the center comes out clean, about 45 minutes. Let cool on a wire rack. Reduce oven temperature to 325°.
4. In a large bowl, beat egg whites, almond extract, remaining ½ cup sugar, and remaining ½ teaspoon vanilla with a mixer at high speed until soft peaks form. Top bread pudding with meringue mixture.
5. Bake until lightly browned, 5 to 6 minutes. Serve warm or cooled.

COOKING TIP FROM MAMA JEN

Happiness is cooking with friends and family and all eating together.

BANANA BREAD

MAKES 1 (9X5-INCH) LOAF

Baked with crunchy pecans and a little bit of spice, this sweet bread is the perfect treat to take to friends and neighbors—no special event required.

- ⅔ cup granulated sugar
- ⅓ cup firmly packed light brown sugar
- ¼ cup unsalted butter, melted
- 2 large eggs
- 1 large egg yolk
- 1½ cups mashed ripe bananas (about 4 large)
- ⅓ cup sour cream
- 2 cups all-purpose flour
- ½ cup toasted chopped pecans
- 1 teaspoon Slap Ya Mama Original Blend Cajun Seasoning
- ¾ teaspoon baking soda
- ½ teaspoon baking powder
- 2½ tablespoons Kiss Ya Mama Cinnamon Sugar

1. Preheat oven to 350°. Spray a 9x5-inch loaf pan with baking spray with flour. Line pan with parchment paper, letting excess extend over sides of pan.
2. In a large bowl, whisk together granulated sugar, brown sugar, melted butter, eggs, and egg yolk. Whisk in mashed banana and sour cream.
3. In a medium bowl, whisk together flour, pecans, Slap Ya Mama Original Blend Cajun Seasoning, baking soda, and baking powder. Gradually add flour mixture to sugar mixture, stirring until combined. Spread batter into prepared pan. Sprinkle with Kiss Ya Mama Cinnamon Sugar.
4. Bake for 35 minutes. Rotate pan, and bake until a wooden pick inserted in center comes out clean, 25 to 32 minutes more, covering with foil during final 15 minutes if needed to prevent excess browning. Let cool in pan on a wire rack for 10 minutes. Remove from pan, and let cool on wire rack for 10 minutes. Serve warm or cooled.

BROOKIES AND BEST CHOCOLATE CHIP COOKIES

Slap Ya Mama Brookies are a deliciously spiced dessert and sure to please everyone. A cross between a brownie and a cookie, these brookies have a cookie-like exterior with a soft, chewy brownie-like interior. Best Chocolate Chip Cookies have just a touch of spice, but you can always add more. Give 'em a try—you won't be disappointed.

BROOKIES
MAKES ABOUT 20

- 2 cups semisweet chocolate chunks
- 1 tablespoon canola oil
- 1 teaspoon Slap Ya Mama Hot Blend Cajun Seasoning
- 1 teaspoon unsalted butter
- 2 large eggs, lightly beaten
- ¾ cup firmly packed light brown sugar
- 1 teaspoon ground cinnamon
- ½ teaspoon vanilla extract
- ½ cup all-purpose flour
- ¼ teaspoon baking powder

1. Preheat oven to 350°. Spray 2 baking sheets with cooking spray.
2. In the top of a double boiler, combine chocolate, oil, Slap Ya Mama Hot Blend Cajun Seasoning, and butter. Cook over simmering water until chocolate is melted and mixture is smooth. Set aside, and let cool.
3. In a large bowl, stir together eggs, brown sugar, cinnamon, and vanilla until well combined. Fold in melted chocolate mixture.
4. In a medium bowl, whisk together flour and baking powder. Stir flour mixture into chocolate mixture until combined. Spread mixture into a shallow pan. Freeze until slightly hardened, 5 to 7 minutes.
5. Using a 1-tablespoon scoop, scoop dough, and place 2 inches apart on prepared pans.
6. Bake until tops look dry and cracked, 10 to 12 minutes. Let cool slightly.

BEST CHOCOLATE CHIP COOKIES
MAKES ABOUT 20

- ¾ cup unsalted butter, softened
- ¾ cup granulated sugar
- ¾ cup firmly packed light brown sugar
- 1 large egg
- 1 tablespoon vanilla extract
- 2 cups all-purpose flour
- ½ teaspoon baking soda
- ½ teaspoon Slap Ya Mama Original Blend Cajun Seasoning
- 2 cups semisweet chocolate chips
- 1 cup toasted pecans, chopped

1. In a large bowl, beat butter and sugars with a mixer at medium speed until fluffy, 3 to 4 minutes, stopping to scrape sides of bowl. Add egg, beating until combined. Beat in vanilla.
2. In a medium bowl, whisk together flour, baking soda, and Slap Ya Mama Original Blend Cajun Seasoning. With mixer on low speed, gradually add flour mixture to butter mixture, beating until well combined. Add chocolate and pecans, beating just until combined. Cover dough with plastic wrap, and refrigerate for at least 30 minutes.
3. Preheat oven to 325°. Line baking sheets with parchment paper.
4. Drop dough by heaping tablespoonfuls 3 inches apart onto prepared pans.
5. Bake until edges are lightly browned, about 15 minutes. Using a spatula, gently flatten cookies. Let cool completely on wire racks.

BLACKBERRY SWEET DOUGH PIE

MAKES 1 (9-INCH) PIE

Fresh blackberries, orange zest, and traditional sweet dough make up this comforting pie.

- 6 cups fresh blackberries, divided
- 1 cup granulated sugar
- 3 tablespoons cornstarch
- 5 tablespoons water, divided
- 2 teaspoons orange zest
- 1 teaspoon Slap Ya Mama Original Blend Cajun Seasoning
- 2 tablespoons unsalted butter
- ¼ teaspoon almond extract
- Sweet Dough (recipe follows)
- 1 large egg
- 1½ tablespoons turbinado sugar

1. In a medium saucepan, combine 2 cups blackberries and granulated sugar; cook over medium heat. Slightly muddle blackberries, and stir until mixture comes to a boil. Reduce heat to medium-low, and simmer, stirring frequently, until sugar is dissolved, about 5 minutes.
2. In a medium bowl, combine cornstarch and 3 tablespoons water. Whisk cooked blackberry mixture into cornstarch mixture. Return blackberry mixture to pan, and add zest and Slap Ya Mama Original Blend Cajun Seasoning; cook, stirring constantly, until mixture boils and thickens, about 1 minute. Remove from heat; add butter and extract, and stir until butter is melted.
3. In a large bowl, place remaining 4 cups blackberries. Gently stir in blackberry mixture. Set aside, and let cool to room temperature.
4. Preheat oven to 400°. Line a 9-inch pie pan with parchment paper.
5. On a heavily floured surface, roll Sweet Dough into a 12-inch circle. Transfer to prepared pan, pressing into bottom and up sides. Fill with blackberry mixture. Fold dough edges in toward center of pie, cutting as needed to fit.
6. In a small bowl, whisk together egg and remaining 2 tablespoons water. Lightly brush dough with egg wash. Sprinkle with turbinado sugar. Place pie on a baking sheet.
7. Bake until lightly browned, 25 to 30 minutes. Let cool on pan for 5 minutes. Remove from baking sheet, and let cool completely in pie pan on a wire rack.

SWEET DOUGH

MAKES 1 (9-INCH) CRUST

- ¼ cup unsalted butter, softened
- 2 tablespoons lard
- ¾ cup granulated sugar
- 1 large egg
- 2½ cups all-purpose flour
- 1 teaspoon baking powder
- ¼ teaspoon Slap Ya Mama Original Blend Cajun Seasoning
- ⅓ cup whole milk

1. In a large bowl, beat butter, lard, and sugar with a mixer at medium speed until fluffy, 3 to 4 minutes, stopping to scrape sides of bowl. Add egg, beating well.
2. In a medium bowl, sift together flour, baking powder, and Slap Ya Mama Original Blend Cajun Seasoning. With mixer on low speed, gradually add flour mixture to butter mixture alternately with milk, beginning and ending with flour mixture, beating just until combined after each addition. (Do not overmix. Dough will be soft and sticky.)
3. Turn out dough onto a lightly floured surface, and shape into a disk. Wrap in plastic wrap, and refrigerate for at least 2 hours or overnight.

BANANAS FOSTER

MAKES 4 SERVINGS

You only need a few simple ingredients—and your favorite vanilla ice cream—to create a delicious dessert that will knock your socks off.

- ¾ cup unsalted butter
- 2 cups firmly packed light brown sugar
- ½ teaspoon kosher salt
- ¼ teaspoon ground cinnamon
- 5 ripe bananas, cut in half and sliced lengthwise
- ½ cup dark rum
- Vanilla ice cream, to serve

1. In a large skillet, melt butter over medium-high heat. Stir in brown sugar, salt, and cinnamon; cook, stirring constantly, until sugar is dissolved. Add bananas, and cook until tender, about 4 minutes. Remove from heat. Add rum; use a stick lighter to ignite rum. Cook until flames die out. Serve with vanilla ice cream.

COOKING TIP FROM MAMA JEN

A messy kitchen is a sign of a happy cook.

SNICKERDOODLES

MAKES ABOUT 34

Known for their soft, chewy texture and sweet cinnamon-sugar coating, Snickerdoodles are the perfect cookie to enjoy year-round.

- 1 cup unsalted butter, softened
- 1¼ cups granulated sugar
- ½ cup firmly packed light brown sugar
- 2 large eggs, room temperature
- 1½ teaspoons vanilla extract
- 2¾ cups all-purpose flour
- 1½ teaspoons cream of tartar
- 1 teaspoon baking soda
- 1 teaspoon kosher salt
- ½ (5-ounce) container Kiss Ya Mama Cinnamon Sugar

1. Preheat oven to 375°. Line 4 baking sheets with parchment paper.
2. In the bowl of a stand mixer fitted with the paddle attachment, beat butter, granulated sugar, and brown sugar at medium speed until fluffy, 3 to 4 minutes, stopping to scrape sides of bowl. Add eggs, one at a time, beating well after each addition. Beat in vanilla.
3. In a medium bowl, whisk together flour, cream of tartar, baking soda, and salt. With mixer on low speed, gradually add flour mixture to butter mixture, beating until just combined.
4. Pour Kiss Ya Mama Cinnamon Sugar in a small bowl. Using a 1½-tablespoon scoop, scoop dough, and roll into smooth 1½-inch balls. Toss balls in Kiss Ya Mama Cinnamon Sugar until well coated. Place 2 inches apart on prepared pans.
5. Bake, one pan at a time, until edges are lightly golden brown but centers still look slightly wet, 10 to 12 minutes. Let cool on pan for 5 minutes. Remove from pan, and let cool completely on wire racks. Store in an airtight container for up to 3 days.

CANE SYRUP SNAPS

MAKES 30

A gingersnap gets a Louisana makeover with these cookies. With cane syrup and Kiss Ya Mama Cinnamon Sugar, you'll never go back to using just ginger.

- ¾ cup all-vegetable shortening
- 1 cup granulated sugar
- ⅓ cup cane syrup
- 1 large egg
- 2⅓ cups all-purpose flour
- 1 tablespoon ground ginger
- 2 teaspoons baking soda
- 1½ teaspoons Kiss Ya Mama Cinnamon Sugar, plus more for coating
- ½ teaspoon kosher salt
- ½ teaspoon ground cloves

1. Preheat oven to 350°. Line 2 baking sheets with parchment paper.
2. In a large bowl, beat shortening and granulated sugar with a mixer at medium speed until fluffy, 1 to 2 minutes. Add cane syrup, beating until just combined. Add egg, beating until just combined.
3. In a medium bowl, stir together flour, ginger, baking soda, 1½ teaspoons Kiss Ya Mama Cinnamon Sugar, salt, and cloves. With mixer on low speed, gradually add flour mixture to shortening mixture, beating until combined.
4. Pour Kiss Ya Mama Cinnamon Sugar in a small bowl. Using a 1½-tablespoon spring-loaded scoop, scoop dough, and roll into balls. Toss balls in Kiss Ya Mama Cinnamon Sugar until well coated. Place at least 1½ inches apart on prepared baking sheets.
5. Bake until golden brown and the edges are set, 12 to 15 minutes. Let cool on pans for 5 minutes. Remove from pans, and let cool completely on wire racks.

CINNAMON SUGAR POUND CAKE

MAKES 1 (10-CUP) BUNDT CAKE

A delicious vanilla pound cake is brushed with butter and dusted with Kiss Ya Mama Cinnamon Sugar. Enjoy with a cup of coffee for an afternoon treat.

- ¾ cup unsalted butter, softened
- 1¼ cups granulated sugar
- ¼ cup firmly packed light brown sugar
- 4 large eggs, room temperature
- 2¾ cups cake flour
- 2 teaspoons baking powder
- 1 teaspoon kosher salt
- ½ teaspoon baking soda
- 1¼ cups whole Greek yogurt, room temperature
- ⅓ cup whole milk, room temperature
- 1 tablespoon vanilla extract
- 2 tablespoons unsalted butter, melted
- ½ (5-ounce) container Kiss Ya Mama Cinnamon Sugar, plus more for sprinkling

1. Preheat oven to 350°.

2. In the bowl of a stand mixer fitted with the paddle attachment, beat softened butter, granulated sugar, and brown sugar at medium speed until fluffy, 3 to 4 minutes, stopping to scrape sides of bowl. Add eggs, one at a time, beating well after each addition. (Mixture may be slightly curdled, but batter will come together.)

3. In a medium bowl, whisk together flour, baking powder, salt, and baking soda. In a small bowl, whisk together yogurt, milk, and vanilla. With mixer on low speed, gradually add flour mixture to butter mixture alternately with yogurt mixture, beginning and ending with flour mixture, beating just until combined after each addition. (Batter will be thick.)

4. Spray a 10-cup Bundt pan with baking spray with flour.

5. Spoon batter into prepared pan. Tap pan on counter several times to spread batter into grooves and release any air bubbles. Using a small offset spatula, smooth top, pushing batter into sides of pan.

6. Bake until a wooden pick inserted near center comes out clean, 50 to 55 minutes. Let cool in pan for 10 minutes. Loosen cake from center of pan using a small offset spatula. Invert cake pan onto a wire rack placed over a rimmed baking sheet; let stand in pan for 10 minutes. Remove pan, and let cake cool completely.

7. Brush cake with melted butter, and cover with Kiss Ya Mama Cinnamon Sugar, pressing gently to adhere. Store in an airtight container for up to 3 days.

CINNAMON SWEET POTATO CAKE

MAKES 1 (9-INCH) CAKE

A soft, moist cake is topped with a cream cheese frosting for a delicious fall dessert.

- ½ cup unsalted butter, softened
- ¾ cup granulated sugar
- ½ cup firmly packed light brown sugar
- 2 large eggs, room temperature
- 1 cup mashed baked sweet potato (see Note)
- 2 teaspoons vanilla extract
- 1½ cups all-purpose flour
- 1 teaspoon baking powder
- 1½ teaspoons Kiss Ya Mama Cinnamon Sugar, plus more for garnish
- ½ teaspoon kosher salt
- ½ teaspoon ground ginger
- ½ teaspoon ground black pepper
- ¼ teaspoon baking soda
- ½ cup whole buttermilk, room temperature
- Cream Cheese Frosting (recipe follows)

1. Preheat oven to 350°. Spray a 9-inch round baking pan with baking spray with flour. Line pan with parchment paper.

2. In the bowl of a stand mixer fitted with the paddle attachment, beat butter, granulated sugar, and brown sugar at medium speed until fluffy, 3 to 4 minutes, stopping to scrape sides of bowl. Add eggs, one at a time, beating well after each addition. Add sweet potato and vanilla, and beat just until combined. (Batter may look broken at first. That's OK. It will come together.)

3. In a medium bowl, whisk together flour, baking powder, Kiss Ya Mama Cinnamon Sugar, salt, ginger, pepper, and baking soda. With mixer on low speed, gradually add flour mixture to butter mixture alternately with buttermilk, beginning and ending with flour mixture, beating until just combined after each addition. Spread batter into prepared pan.

4. Bake until a wooden pick inserted in center comes out clean, 45 to 50 minutes. Let cool in pan on wire rack for 30 minutes. Remove cake from pan, and let cool completely on wire rack.

5. Top with Cream Cheese Frosting. Garnish with Kiss Ya Mama Cinnamon Sugar, if desired. Serve immediately. Refrigerate in an airtight container for up to 3 days.

Note: To bake sweet potato, pierce 2 medium sweet potatoes with a fork and wrap each in foil. Bake at 400° until fork tender, about 1 hour.

CREAM CHEESE FROSTING

MAKES ABOUT 2 CUPS

- 8 ounces cream cheese, softened
- ¼ cup unsalted butter, softened
- ¼ teaspoon kosher salt
- 1 teaspoon vanilla extract
- 3½ cups confectioners' sugar

1. In the bowl of a stand mixer fitted with the paddle attachment, beat cream cheese at medium speed until creamy, 2 to 3 minutes. Beat in butter until smooth and combined. Beat in salt and vanilla. Gradually add confectioners' sugar, beating until smooth. Beat at high speed until frosting is light and fluffy, 2 to 3 minutes. Use immediately.

APPLE HAND PIES

MAKES ABOUT 12

The Walker kids love these hand pies. It's the perfect grab-and-go dessert for sweet lovers at any age.

- 2 tablespoons unsalted butter
- 3 cups diced peeled sweet firm apple (about 2 large apples)
- ½ cup firmly packed light brown sugar
- 1 tablespoon fresh lemon juice
- 1 teaspoon vanilla extract
- ½ (5-ounce) container plus ½ teaspoon Kiss Ya Mama Cinnamon Sugar
- ¼ teaspoon kosher salt
- 3½ teapoons cornstarch
- 4 tablespoons water, divided
- Pie Dough (recipe follows)
- Vegetable oil, for frying

1. In a medium saucepan, melt butter over medium heat. Stir in apple, brown sugar, lemon juice, vanilla, ½ teaspoon Kiss Ya Mama Cinnamon Sugar, and salt. Cook, stirring frequently, until apples are soft, 3 to 4 minutes.

2. In a small bowl, whisk together cornstarch and 1 tablespoon water. Add to apple mixture, and cook, stirring constantly, until mixture is thick and translucent, 2 to 3 minutes. Remove from heat, and let cool completely.

3. On a lightly floured surface, roll Pie Dough out to ⅛-inch thickness. Using a 4-inch round cutter, cut 12 rounds from dough, rerolling once if needed. Line a baking sheet with parchment paper.

4. Place 1½ tablespoons apple mixture in center of each round. Brush edges of rounds with remaining water. Fold dough over filling. Using a fork, crimp edges to seal. Place pies on prepared baking sheet. Refrigerate until firm, at least 20 minutes.

5. In a large heavy-bottomed saucepan, pour oil to a depth of 1½ inches, and heat over medium heat until a deep-fry thermometer registers 365°. Line a rimmed baking sheet with paper towels. Pour remaining ½ container Kiss Ya Mama Cinnamon Sugar into a bowl.

6. Working in batches, gently lower hand pies into oil. Fry until crust is golden, 3 to 4 minutes. Use a spider strainer or a slotted spoon to transfer pies to prepare baking sheets. Let pies cool for at least 5 minutes. While still warm, toss pies in Kiss Ya Mama Cinnamon Sugar. Let pies cool for at least 5 minutes. Best served warm.

PIE DOUGH

MAKES DOUGH FOR 12 HAND PIES

- 2¼ cups all-purpose flour
- 1½ teaspoons kosher salt
- ¾ cup cold unsalted butter, cut into ½-inch cubes
- ¼ cup ice water, plus more as needed

1. In the work bowl of a food processor, place flour and salt; pulse until combined. Add cold butter, and pulse until mixture is crumbly and butter is in pea-size pieces. With processor running, add ¼ cup ice water in a slow, steady stream just until dough comes together. (Mixture may appear crumbly. It should be moist and hold together when pinched.) Add more ice water as needed.

2. Turn out dough, and press into a flat disk. Wrap tightly in plastic wrap. Refrigerate for at least 1 hour, or up to 2 days. After 2 days, dough can be kept in the freezer for up to 3 months. If using from frozen, let thaw in the fridge overnight.

MAMA RUTH'S FUDGE

MAKES ABOUT 20 SERVINGS

Once you've had Mama Ruth's chocolate fudge, no other chocolate fudge will compare. It's full of pecans for a delightful creamy, crunchy bite.

- 5 cups granulated sugar
- 5 cups whole milk
- 3 cups chopped pecans
- 1 cup evaporated milk
- 5 teaspoons cocoa powder
- 4 tablespoons margarine or unsalted butter

1. In a tall-sided large pot, stir together all ingredients. Bring to a hard boil over medium-high heat, stirring constantly, until it turns into a ball. (Test by dropping a small amount of mixture into a cup of cold water. If you're able to roll it between your fingers into a ball, it's ready. Alternatively, cook until an instant-read thermometer registers 240°.)

2. Fill a sink with enough water to cover bottom of pot. Place pot in water. Continue to stir mixture until it makes a crackling sound, about 3 to 5 minutes. Spread into a greased 12x8-inch pan. Let cool completely before cutting.

COOKING TIP FROM MAMA RUTH

Make sure to stir mixture constantly. If left unattended, it can boil over.

MAMA JEN'S PEANUT BUTTER FUDGE

MAKES ABOUT 20 SERVINGS

Mama Jen's fudge is legendary in the Walker family. Everyone wants their own gift tub every holiday season. It's that good!

- 2 teaspoons unsalted butter
- 3 cups granulated sugar
- 1 cup evaporated milk
- 1¼ cups peanut butter
- 1½ teaspoons vanilla extract
- ¼ teaspoon cream of tarter

1. In a tall-sided large pot, melt butter over medium heat. Add sugar and evaporated milk. Bring to a boil, and boil for 2 minutes. Remove from heat. Stir in peanut butter, vanilla and cream of tartar until well combined. Spread mixture into a greased 8-inch baking pan and refrigerate until set. Once firm, cut into squares and serve.

RECIPE INDEX

APPETIZERS
Bloody Mary Pickled Shrimp 63
Boudin Rolls with Spicy
    Cane Syrup 70
Brie & Bacon Oysters 49
Buffalo Chicken Wings 65
Cajun Meat Pies 61
Crab Cakes 51
Crab Dip 55
Crawfish Bread Bowl Dip 59
Crawfish Hand Pies 60
Deviled Eggs 47
Fried Boudin Balls 41
Grattons 67
Green Tomato Salsa 73
Mama Jen's Cajun Cornbread 45
Mama Jen's Shrimp Dip 55
New Orleans Barbecue Oysters ... 49
Paw Paw Dub's Hot Dip 57
Savory Sweet Potato Hand Pies ... 74
Spinach & Andouille Oysters 49
Stuffed Bell Peppers 43
Stuffed Jalapeños Wrapped in
    Bacon 53
Sweet Potato Cheese Fries with
    Debris 69

BREAKFAST
Beignets 28
Bloody Mary Board 26
Cinnamon Sugar Donuts 22
Classic Cinnamon Rolls 32
Crawfish-Potato Omelet 18
Creole Tomato Breakfast
    Sandwiches 30
Kiss Ya Mama Muffins 36
Pain Perdu 34
Paw Paw Bev's Biscuits 24

DESSERTS
Apple Hand Pies 247
Banana Bread 231
Bananas Foster 237
Best Chocolate Chip Cookies .. 233
Blackberry Sweet Dough Pie .. 235
Bread Pudding 229
Brookies 233
Cane Syrup Snaps 241
Cinnamon Sugar Pound Cake .. 243
Cinnamon Sweet Potato
    Cake 245
Mama Jen's Peanut Butter
    Fudge 251
Mama Ruth's Fudge 249
Maw Maw's Pecan Pie 227
Snickerdoodles 239

ENTRÉES
BBQ Shrimp 132
Beef Pot Roast 163
Blackened Redfish 136
Boiled Crabs 148
Boiled Shrimp 148
Cajun Fried Turkey 191
Cajun Roasted Chicken 177
Catfish Courtbouillon 140
Chicken Gumbo Casserole 195
Chicken Sauce Piquante 161
Crawfish Boil 144
Crawfish Étouffée 130
Crispy Cajun-Fried Alligator ... 150
Crunchy Catfish Tacos with
    Apple Slaw 152
Fried Catfish with Crawfish
    au Gratin 138
Fried Pork Chops 181
Grilled Pork Ribs 193
Holiday Ham 175
Jambalaya 165
Maw Maw's Fried Chicken 171
Maw Maw's Red Beans & Rice .. 165
Meatball Stew 179
Pastalaya 173
Ponce Sauce Piquante 159

Pork Chop Stew 189
Pot-Roasted Whole Duck 185
Shrimp & Grits 134
Shrimp Fettuccine 146
Squirrel Sauce Piquante 169
Stuffed Wild Duck Breast 183
Venison Sauce Piquante 187

SANDWICHES AND PO' BOYS
Blackened Grouper
    Sandwiches 127
Cajun Burgers 121
Debris Po' Boys 115
Fried Catfish Po' Boys 113
Fried Chicken Club
    Sandwiches 117
Fried Shrimp Po' Boys 111
Muffulettas 119
Spicy Bacon and Poblano Grilled
    Cheese 123
Steak Sandwiches 125

SAUCES AND MISCELLANEOUS
Apple Slaw 153
Black Cherry Sauce 183
Cajun Butter 123
Cajun Pecans 214
Candied Pecans 202
C'est Bon Slaw 117
Cream Cheese Frosting 245
Dark Flour 82
Dark Roux 179
Mama Jen's Cajun Crawfish
    Dipping Sauce 144
Mama Jen's Spicy Cajun Seafood
    Dipping Sauce 145
Pie Dough 75, 247
Rémoulade Sauce 111
Sour Cream-Lime Sauce 75
Spicy Cane Syrup 71
Sweet Dough 235

SIDES
Black-Eyed Peas and Sausage .. 220
Candied Yams & Pecans 202

Classic Collard Greens 210
Corn Tasso Maque Choux 218
Cornbread Dressing 200
Crawfish Mac & Cheese 204
Dirty Rice Dressing................... 200
Field Pea Caviar 216
Green Bean Casserole............. 208
Louisiana Oyster Dressing........ 222
Parmesan Grilled Corn.............. 212
Roasted Asparagus with Cajun
    Pecans 214
Roasted Brussels Sprouts......... 206
World-Famous Slap Ya Mama
    Atomic Potatoes 198

SOUPS & SALADS
Chicken & Sausage Gumbo........ 87
Creamy Sweet Potato Soup 102
French Onion Soup 90
Fried Oysters Salad 84
Grilled Vegetables and Zesty
    Rice Salad 106
Hearty Beef & Bean Chili........... 96
Homemade Vegetable Soup 92
Mama Jen's Potato Salad 98
Pickled Okra Succotash
    Salad.................................. 104
Seafood Gumbo 78
Shrimp & Corn Soup with
    Tasso 80
Skirt Steak Salad......................... 94
Smoky Chicken Salad 100
Summer Okra & Tomato
    Salad.................................... 88
Turtle Soup 82

CREDITS
Family photo (page 12) courtesy of Jacqueline Clair Photography.

ACKNOWLEDGMENTS

We would like to send a heartfelt thank-you to the following for making this cookbook and so much more possible.

Thank you to our friends and family for their continued support, their relentless promotion of Slap Ya Mama, and the many hours testing new products with us. You have no idea how much we appreciate everything you do for us. Thank you!

Thank you to 83 Press and their entire team. Without your help and guidance, this cookbook would still be just an idea rattling around in our heads.

Thank you to Ville Platte, Evangeline Parish, the entire Acadiana area, and every Cajun around this world. Your love for our unique culture helps fuel our desire to share all we have to offer. We will forever be proud to be Cajuns, and with your help, we hope to spread that joy all over the world.

Thank you to our co-packers who help us bring the flavor; the distributors who took a chance on a little company from Ville Platte, Louisiana; our local banking institutions that let us borrow money when we only had a dream; the marketing agencies that help us get creative; and to all those who helped teach us the distribution and grocery business. It has been a wild adventure, and we look forward to many more years of working with you.

Thank you to our customers from all over the world. It's fans such as yourselves who keep us motivated to create new products and allow us to share our love of food with the world. We are forever grateful for all your support and love. Thank you for helping make our dream come true.

Finally, thank you to God. Without You, none of this is possible; all glory be to You.